D0089048

# The Little Book
# That Beats the Market

# The Little Book
# That Beats the Market

Joel Greenblatt

WILEY

John Wiley & Sons, Inc.

Published by John Wiley & Sons, Inc., Hoboken, New Jersey
Published simultaneously in Canada

For general information on our other products and services or for technical support,
please contact our Customer Care Department within the United States at (800)
762-2974, outside the United States at (317) 572-3993 or fax (317) 572-4002.

Wiley also publishes its books in a variety of electronic formats. Some content that
appears in print may not be available in electronic books. For more information
about Wiley products, visit our web site at www.wiley.com.

ISBN-13 978-0-471-73306-5
ISBN-10 0-471-73306-7

Printed in the United States of America

10 9 8 7 6 5

To my wonderful wife, Julie,
and our five magnificent spin-offs

# Contents

# Acknowledgments

I am grateful to the many friends, colleagues, and family who have contributed to this project. In particular, special thanks are due to my partners at Gotham Capital, Rob Goldstein and John Petry. Not only are they the true coauthors of the *Magic Formula* study that appears in this book, but it is also a rare privilege to be associated with such brilliant, talented, and generous people. Their contributions to this book—and to the success of Gotham Capital—cannot be overstated and are appreciated more than they know. I would also like to give special thanks to Edward Ramsden at Caburn Capital for his extraordinarily insightful comments, suggestions, and editing work; to Norbert Lou at Punchcard Capital, particularly for his inspiration and suggestions for Chapter 9; and to Patrick Ede at Gotham Capital for his major contributions to the *Magic Formula* study, for his intelligent and helpful comments, and for his editing talents. In addition, my brother, Richard Greenblatt at America Capital, deserves a major part of the credit for being my editor-at-large, for his many good ideas, for his numerous contributions to each chapter, and especially for his encouragement with this project and throughout my life.

I am also grateful for the many helpful contributions and inspiration provided by Dr. Sharon Curhan (my sister, and my favorite artist), Dr. Gary Curhan, Joshua Curhan, Justin Curhan, Linda Greenblatt Gordon at Saddle Rock Partners, Michael Gordon, Bryan Binder at Caxton Associates, Dr. Susan Binder, Allan and Mickey Greenblatt (my wonderful parents), Dr. George and Cecile Teebor (the famous in-laws), Ezra Merkin at Gabriel Capital, Rod Moskowitz, John Scully, Marc Silbert, David Rabinowitz at Kirkwood Capital, Larry Balaban, Rabbi Label Lam, Eric Rosenfeld at Crescendo Partners, Robert Kushel (my broker at Smith Barney), Dan Nir at Gracie Capital, Brian Gaines at Springhouse Capital, Bruce Newberg (who got me started), Matthew Newberg, and Rich Pzena at Pzena Investment Management. Special thanks to David Pugh, my editor at John Wiley, and Sandra Dijkstra, my literary agent, for their encouragement and enthusiastic support of this project. Thank you also to Andrew Tobias for graciously writing the foreword and for being a good friend.

I would also like to thank my two oldest children, Matthew and Rebecca Greenblatt, for being willing students and readers (and for laughing at most of the jokes). To my three youngest children, thank you for your inspiration. And to all the kids, thank you for the joy you bring each day. Thank you also to my beautiful wife, Julie, for her sage advice with this book, and in life, for her love and support and for each precious day together.

# Foreword

The best thing about this book—from which I intend to steal liberally for the next edition of *The Only Investment Guide You'll Ever Need*—is that most people won't believe it. Or, believing it, won't have the patience to follow its advice. That's good, because the more people who know about a good thing, the more expensive that thing ordinarily becomes . . . bye-bye bargain.

Yet unlike most "systems" meant to exploit anomalies in the market, Joel Greenblatt's simple notion will likely retain at least a good deal of its validity even if it becomes widely followed.

I don't want to spoil the surprise—the book is short enough as it is. My role here is simply to introduce you to the author, so you have some sense of just how far you can trust him.

I've known Joel for decades. He is really smart, really modest, really well intentioned and—here is the unusual part—really successful. (I mean: *really* successful.)

More to the point, his success has come from shrewd investing (not from selling books).

He is also funny. I read the first couple of chapters of this book to my 11-year-old nephew, Timmy, and we both enjoyed it. Timmy, with no investable funds that I know of, then fell asleep as I raced to the end, mentally rejiggering my retirement plan.

Let me tell you this much: In the beginning, there were mutual funds, and that was good. But their sales fees and expenses were way too high. Then came no-load funds, which were better. They eliminated the sales fee, but were still burdened with management fees and with the tax and transactional burden that comes from active management. Then came "index funds," which cut fees, taxes, and transaction costs to the bone. Very, very good.

What Joel would have you consider, in effect, is an index-fund-plus, where the "plus" comes from including in *your* basket of stocks only good businesses selling at low valuations. And he has an easy way for you to find them.

Not everyone can beat the averages, of course—by definition. But my guess is that patient people who follow Joel's advice will beat them over time. And that if millions of people *should* adopt this strategy (Vanguard: please hurry up and offer a low-priced fund like this), two things will happen. First, the advantage of investing this way will diminish but not disappear. Second, stock market valuations will become ever so slightly more rational, making our capital allocation process ever so slightly more efficient.

Not bad work for a skinny little book.

Now, gather ye what 11-year-olds ye may, and dive in.

—Andrew Tobias, author of
*The Only Investment Guide You'll Ever Need*

# Introduction

This book was originally inspired by my desire to give each of my five children a gift. I figured if I could teach them how to make money for themselves, then I would be giving them a great gift—truly one that would keep giving. I also figured that if I could explain how to make money in terms that even my kids could understand (the ones already in sixth and eighth grades, anyway), then I could pretty much teach anyone how to be a successful stock market investor.

While the concepts covered in this book may seem simple—perhaps too simple for sophisticated investors—each step along the way is there for a reason. Stay with it, and I assure you the payoff for both beginning and experienced investors will be huge.

After more than 25 years of investing professionally and after 9 years of teaching at an Ivy League business school, I am convinced of at least two things:

1. If you really want to "beat the market," most professionals and academics can't help you, and
2. That leaves only one real alternative: You must *do it yourself.*

Luckily, that might not be such a bad thing. As improbable as it may seem, you *can* learn to beat the market. Through a simple, step-by-step process, this book can teach you how. To help you along, I have included a *magic formula.* The formula is simple, it makes perfect sense, and with it, you can beat the market, the professionals, and the academics by a wide margin. And you can do it with low risk. The formula has worked for many years and will continue to work even after everyone knows it. Although the formula is easy to use and will not take much of your time, it will work for *you* only if you make the effort to fully understand *why* it works.

Along the way, you will learn:

- How to view the stock market
- Why success eludes almost all individual and professional investors
- How to find *good* companies at *bargain* prices
- How you can beat the market all by yourself

I have included an Appendix section for those of you with a higher level of financial training, but it is not necessary for people to read or understand the appendixes to be able to understand and apply the methods found in this book. The truth is that you don't need an MBA to beat the market. Knowing lots of sophisticated formulas or financial terms isn't what makes the difference. Understanding the simple concepts in this book . . . *is*.

So please enjoy this gift. May the small investment of time (and 20 bucks or so) greatly enrich your future. Good luck.

# Chapter One

JASON'S IN THE SIXTH GRADE, and he's making a fortune. My son and I see him almost every day on the way to school. There's Jason in the back of his chauffeur-driven limousine, all decked out in cool clothes and dark sunglasses. Ahhh, to be 11 years old, rich, and cool. Now that's the life. Okay, maybe I'm getting a little carried away. I mean, it's not really a limousine; it's kind of a scooter. And the cool clothes and sunglasses part, well, that's not really true, either. It's more like his belly hanging over a pair of jeans, no sunglasses, and what he had for breakfast still stuck to his face. But that's not my point. Jason's in business.

It's a simple business, but it works. Jason buys gum, four or five packs a day. It's 25 cents for a pack and five sticks of gum to a package. According to my son, once in school, Jason transforms himself into a superhero of sorts. Neither rain nor sleet nor evil hall monitors can keep Jason from selling his gum. I guess his customers like buying from a superhero (or maybe they're just stuck in school), but however he does it, Jason sells each stick of gum for 25 cents. (Supposedly—I've never actually seen it myself—Jason kind of shoves an open pack of gum into a potential customer's face and repeats "You want some, you know you want some!" until his fellow student either collapses or forks over a quarter.)

The way my son has it figured, that's five sticks at 25 cents each, so Jason rakes in $1.25 for each pack he sells. At a cost of 25 cents per pack, that means Jason is making $1 of pure profit on every pack he can shove . . . I mean, sell. At four or five packs a day, that's a lot of money! So after one of our daily Jason sightings, I asked *my* sixth-grader, "Gee, how much do you think this guy Jason can make by the end of high school?" My son—we'll call him Ben (even though his real name is Matt)—started whizzing through the calculations using all his brainpower (and a few fingers). "Let's see," he replied. "That's, say, four bucks a day, times five days a week. So, $20 a week, 36 weeks of school, that's $720 a year. If he has six years left until he graduates, that's somewhere over $4,000 more he'll make by the end of high school!"

Not wanting to miss an opportunity to teach, I asked, "Ben, if Jason offered to sell you half of his business, how much would you pay? In other words, he'll share half his profits from the gum business with you over the six years until he graduates, but he wants you to give him money now. How much would you give him?"

"Well . . ."—I could see Ben's wheels start to turn now that there might be some real money on the line— "maybe Jason doesn't sell four or five packs a day, but three packs—that's a pretty safe bet. So maybe he makes three bucks a day. That's still $15 in a five-day school week. So, 36 weeks in a school year, that's 36 times 15 (I might have helped a little in here), that's over $500 a year. Jason has six more years of school, so 6 times $500 is $3,000 by the time he graduates!"

"Okay," I said, "so I guess you'd pay Jason $1,500 for half of those profits, right?"

"No way," Ben answered quickly. "First, why should I pay $1,500 to get back $1,500? That doesn't make any sense. Besides, the $1,500 I get from Jason will take six years to collect. Why would I give him $1,500 now to get back $1,500 over six years? Also, maybe Jason does a little better than I figure and I get more than $1,500, but he could do worse, too!"

"Yeah," I chimed in, "maybe other kids start to sell gum in school, and Jason has so much competition he can't sell as much."

"Nah, Jason's practically a superhero," Ben says. "I don't think anyone can sell as well as Jason, so I'm not too worried about that."

"So I see your point," I responded. "Jason's got a good business, but $1,500 is too much to pay for half. But what if Jason offered you half his business for $1? Would you buy it then?"

"Of course," Ben shot back with a "Dad, you're being an idiot" kind of tone.

"So, fine," I said, ignoring the tone for a moment. "The right price is somewhere between $1 and $1,500. Now we're getting closer, but how much would you pay?"

"Four hundred fifty bucks. That's how much I'd pay today. If I collected $1,500 over the next six years, I think that would be a good deal," Ben said, evidently pleased with his decision.

"Great!" I responded. "Now you finally understand what I do for a living."

"Dad, what the heck are you talking about? Now I'm totally lost. I've never seen any gum!"

"No, Ben, I don't sell gum. I spend my time figuring out what businesses are worth, just like we did with

Jason's business. If I can buy a business for a lot less than I think it's worth, I buy it!"

"Wait a second," blurted out Ben. "That sounds too easy. If a business is worth $1,000, why would anyone sell it to you for $500?"

Well, as it turned out, Ben's seemingly reasonable and obvious question was actually the magic question that got this whole project started. I told Ben that he had just asked a great question, that believe it or not, there is a place where they sell businesses at half price all the time. I told him that I could teach him where to look and how to buy those bargains for himself. But, of course, I told him there was a catch.

The catch isn't that the answer is incredibly complicated. It's not. The catch isn't that you have to be some kind of genius or superspy to find $1,000 bills selling for $500. You don't. In fact, I decided to write this book so that Ben and his siblings could not only understand what I do for a living but also so that they could learn how to start finding these bargain investments for themselves. I figure whatever career they choose in the future (even if it's not money management, a career I'm not necessarily encouraging), they'll definitely need to learn how to invest some of their earnings.

But, like I told Ben, there is a catch. The catch is that you have to listen to a long story, you have to take the time to understand the story, and most important, you have to actually *believe* that the story is true. In fact, the story even concludes with a magic formula that can make you rich over time. I kid you not. Unfortunately, if you don't believe the magic formula will make you rich, it won't. On the other hand, if you believe the story I'm going to tell you—I mean really, truly believe—then you can choose to make money with or without the formula. (The formula will take significantly less time and effort than doing the "work" yourself, and will provide better results for most people, but you can decide which way to go when you're done reading.)

Okay, I know what you're thinking. What's this *belief* stuff about? Are we talking about a new religion, maybe something to do with *Peter Pan* or *The Wizard of Oz*? (I won't even bring up the witch-inside-the-crystal-ball thing that still scares the heck out of me, or the flying monkeys, mainly because neither has anything to do with my story.) And what about the getting *rich* part, what's that? Can a book really teach you how to get rich? That doesn't make sense. If it could, everyone would be rich. That's especially true for a book that claims to have a magic formula. If everyone knows the magic formula and everyone can't be rich, pretty soon the formula will have to stop working.

But I told you this was a long story. I'm going to start from the very beginning. For my kids and most others, almost all of this stuff will be new. For adults, even if they think they know a lot about investing already, even if they've been to graduate business school, and even if they manage other people's money professionally, most have learned wrong. And they've learned wrong from the beginning. Very few people really believe the story I'm going to tell. I know this because if they did—if they really, truly did—there would be a lot more successful investors out there. There aren't. I believe I can teach you (and each of my children) to be one of them. So let's get started.

# Chapter Two

ACTUALLY, JUST GETTING STARTED is a big deal. It takes a great amount of discipline to save *any* money. After all, no matter how much money you earn or receive from others, it's simply much easier and more immediately rewarding to find something to spend it on. When I was young, I decided that all *my* money should go to Johnson Smith. Of course, I'd love to tell you that Johnson Smith was an orphan who just needed a little help. I'd love to tell you that the money given to Johnson Smith helped change his life. I'd love to tell you that, but it wouldn't be completely accurate. You see, Johnson Smith was a company. Not just any company, either. It was a company that sold whoopee cushions, itching powder, and imitation dog vomit through the mail.

I mean, I didn't completely throw away all my money. I did buy some educational stuff, too. Once, the guys at Johnson Smith were able to sell me a weather balloon that was 10 feet tall and 30 feet around. I'm not sure what a giant balloon had to do with the weather, but it sounded educational, sort of. Anyway, after my brother and I finally figured out how to blow it up by somehow reversing the airflow on the vacuum cleaner, we ran into a big problem. The 10-foot balloon was quite a bit larger than our front door. Using a complicated formula that not even Einstein could fully comprehend, we decided that if we turned our backs and pushed really hard, the giant balloon could be squeezed out without bursting the balloon or damaging the door (and besides, our mother wasn't home yet). And it worked, except we forgot one thing.

It seems that the air outside was colder than the air inside our house. That meant that we had filled our balloon with warm air. And since, as everyone except apparently me and my brother knew, hot air rises, the balloon started to float away. The two of us were left chasing a giant balloon down the street for about half a mile before it finally popped on a tree.

Luckily, I learned a valuable lesson from the whole experience. Although I don't exactly remember what that was, I'm pretty sure it had something to do with the importance of saving money for things that you might want or need in the future rather than wasting money buying giant weather balloons that you get to chase down the block for all of three or four minutes.

But for our purposes, let's assume that we can all agree that it is important to save money for the future. Let's also assume that you have been able to resist the many temptations of the Johnson Smith people and the thousands of other places calling out for your money; that you (or your parents) have been able to provide for all of the necessities of life, including food, clothing, and shelter; and that by being careful about how much you spend, you have somehow been able to put aside at least a small amount of money. Your challenge is to put that money—let's say $1,000—someplace where it can grow to be even more money.

Sounds simple enough. Sure, you can just put it under your mattress or in your piggy bank, but when you come to get it, even years later, you'll still be left with the same $1,000 you put there in the first place. It won't grow at all. In fact, if the prices of the things you were going to buy with that money go up during the time your money was just sitting there (and therefore your $1,000 will buy less stuff than it used to), your money will actually be worth less than it was worth the day you put it away. In short, the mattress plan kind of stinks.

Plan B has got to be better. And it is. Just take that $1,000 over to the bank. Not only will the bank agree to hold your money, they'll pay *you* for the privilege. Each year, you'll collect *interest* from the bank, and in most cases, the longer you agree to let them hold your money, the higher the interest rate you'll get. If you agree to keep your $1,000 with the bank for five years, you might collect something like 5 percent in interest payments per year. So the first year you collect $50 in interest on your $1,000 original deposit, and now you will have $1,050 in the bank at the beginning of year 2. In year 2, you collect another 5 percent interest on the new, higher total of $1,050, or $52.50 in interest, and so on through year 5. After five years, your $1,000 will grow into $1,276. Not bad, and certainly a lot better than the mattress plan.

Which brings us to Plan C. This plan is known as "who needs the bank?" There's an easy way to just skip the bank altogether and lend to businesses or to a group of individuals yourself. Often businesses borrow money directly by selling *bonds*. The corner bakery won't usually sell these, but larger (multi-million-dollar) companies, such as McDonald's, do it all the time. If you purchase a $1,000 bond from a large company, for example, that company might agree to pay you 8 percent each year and pay back your original $1,000 after 10 years. That clearly beats the crummy 5 percent the bank was willing to pay you.

There's one little problem, though: If you buy a bond from one of these companies and something goes wrong with its business, you may never get your interest or your money back. That's why riskier companies—say, Bob's House of Flapjacks and Pickles—usually have to pay higher interest rates than more solid, established ones. That's why a company's bonds have to pay more than the bank. People need to make more money on their bond to make up for the risk that they may not receive the promised interest rate or their original money back.

Of course, if you're not comfortable taking *any* risk of losing your $1,000, the U.S. government sells bonds, too. While there is nothing completely riskless in this world, lending money to the U.S. government is the closest any of us will ever get. If you are willing to lend the U.S. government your money for 10 years, the government might, for example, agree to pay you something like 6 percent per year (if you lend for shorter periods of time—say, five years—the rate will usually be lower, maybe 4 or 5 percent).

For our purposes, the bond we'll be looking at most is the U.S. government bond that matures (pays off the original loan) after 10 years. We'll be looking at that one because 10 years is a long time. We'll want to compare how much we can earn from a safe bet like a U.S. government bond with our other long-term investment choices. So if the annual interest rate on the 10-year government bond is 6 percent, that essentially means that people who are willing to lend their money out for 10 years, but are unwilling to take any risk of losing their original investment or of not receiving the promised interest rate, can still expect to receive 6 percent each year on their money. In other words, for people willing to lock their money up for 10 years, the "no risk" rate of return is 6 percent per year.

It's important to understand what that means. It means that if anyone asks you to loan them money or to invest with them over the long term, they better expect to pay you more than 6 percent a year. Why? Because you can get 6 percent a year without taking *any* risk. All you have to do is lend money to the U.S. government, and they'll guarantee that you receive your 6 percent each and every year, along with all of your money back after 10 years. If Jason wants money for a share of his gum business, that investment better earn you more than 6 percent per year, or no way should you do it! If Jason wants to borrow money over the long term, same deal. He better expect to pay you a lot more than 6 percent. After all, you can get 6 percent risk free by lending to the U.S. government!

And that's it. There are only a few things you need to remember from this chapter:

## Quick Summary

1. You can stick your money under the mattress. (But that plan kind of stinks.)
2. You can put your money in the bank or buy bonds from the U.S. government. You will be guaranteed an interest rate and your money back with *no risk.**
3. You can buy bonds sold by companies or other groups. You will be promised higher interest rates than you could get by putting your money in the bank or by buying government bonds—*but* you could lose some or all of your money, so you better get paid enough for taking the risk.
4. You can do something else with your money. (We'll talk about what in the next chapter.)

And I almost forgot,

5. Hot air rises.

Hey, I did learn something from that balloon after all. Thanks, Johnson Smith.

*Bank deposits up to $100,000 are guaranteed by an agency of the U.S. government. You must hold your bank deposit or your bond until it matures (possibly 5 or 10 years, depending upon what you buy) to guarantee no loss of your original investment.

I'm going to make your life even simpler. As I write this, the 10-year U.S. government bond rate is substantially lower than 6 percent. However, whenever the long-term government bond is paying less than 6 percent, we will still assume the rate is 6 percent. In other words, our other investment alternatives will, at a minimum, still have to beat 6 percent, no matter how low long-term U.S. government bond interest rates go. The big picture is that we want to make sure we earn a lot more from our other investments than we could earn without taking any risk. Obviously, if long-term U.S. government bond rates rose to 7 percent or higher, we would use 7 percent or that higher number. Now that's really it.

# Chapter Three

**O**KAY. WHAT ELSE CAN YOU DO with your money? Let's face it: Putting money in the bank or lending it to the government is really boring. Hey, *I* know! Why don't we just go to the track and bet it all on a horse! Nah, I actually tried that—didn't work out too well. I even tried the dog races. That's where a bunch of greyhound dogs run around in a circle chasing a little mechanical rabbit. It's fun to watch, and you get to hang out with some really great people. Some of them even have teeth!

You know what, though—on second thought, maybe that's not such a good idea, either. I kind of figured it wasn't for me after *my* dog actually caught the rabbit. My little guy got trampled by the other dogs on the first turn, got up, and started running the wrong way. Unfortunately, the mechanical rabbit zips around the track at about 60 miles an hour, and when my dog, the one I had placed my faith in and my money on, took a flying leap at the rabbit speeding toward him . . . let's just say it wasn't pretty (all right, since you're probably concerned—the dog slammed into the 60-mile-per-hour rabbit at full speed, flew 30 feet in the air, and was tragically disqualified, which meant, alas, I had lost all of my money).*

In any case, now that we've explored most of the logical alternatives for your money (though I'm sure they race worms and various crustaceans some place I haven't found yet), let's look at one more. How about investing in a business? After all, Jason's going to grow up someday. Maybe he'll open up his own gum store. Better yet, maybe he'll open up a whole bunch of gum stores (usually referred to as a "chain" of stores) under some catchy name like Jason's Gum Shops.

Let's assume that Jason personally trains all the salespeople in his unique brand of gum selling and that the chain is wildly successful (it could happen). Now Jason comes to you willing to sell half his business (he wants to buy a new pair of sunglasses, a real limousine, and maybe a house for himself and the lucky Mrs. Jason). Only now

*And yes, the dog was fine.

he's asking for big bucks, and we'll have to do some serious figuring before we can decide whether to take Jason up on his offer.

It turns out that Jason's grown up quite a bit since the days when he scootered himself around town, and he now wants a hefty $6 million for half ownership of his business. Of course, 6 million bucks is more than most of us can afford, but, luckily, Jason isn't looking to sell half ownership of his business all to one person. In fact, Jason has decided to divide ownership of his business into a million equal pieces, or *shares* (as they're referred to on Wall Street). Jason's plan is to keep 500,000 shares for himself and sell his other 500,000 shares for $12 apiece, or $6 million in total. Anyone interested in buying part of Jason's business at that price can buy one share (for $12), a hundred shares (for $1,200), a thousand shares (for $12,000), or pretty much any number of shares they want.

If you were to buy, for example, 10,000 shares costing $120,000, you would then own 1 percent of Jason's Gum Shops (10,000 shares divided by the 1-million-share total). That 1 percent doesn't mean that you would own the spearmint gum department or a small piece of one of Jason's stores. Your 10,000 shares, or 1 percent ownership, of Jason's Gum Shops means that you would be entitled to 1 percent of the future earnings of the entire Jason's Gum Shops business. Now, of course, all you would have to do is figure out whether paying $120,000 for 1 percent of Jason's future gum profits is a good deal. (This is where our analysis gets a little sticky; we have to be good gumshoes so we don't blow it and have our money chewed up and spit out. . . . Anyway, you get the idea.)

Luckily, Jason has provided us with a lot of information. Since we already know that Jason wants $12 for each share in Jason's Gum Shops and that there are 1 million shares in total (this is referred to as 1 million shares *outstanding*), this means that Jason thinks his business is worth $12 million (and therefore he thinks that 1 percent of his business is worth the $120,000 we just talked about). Well, that's all fine and dandy, but what matters here is what *we* think it's worth. So let's take a look at some of the other information Jason has given us.

It seems that last year Jason sold a total of $10 million worth of gum from the 10 stores in the highly successful Jason's Gum Shops chain. Of course, the $10 million is how much gum Jason's stores sold, but unfortunately, $10 million isn't how much profit Jason made. Obviously, Jason's stores ran up a few expenses along the way. Naturally, there was the cost of the gum that Jason sold—that totaled $6 million. That left him with $4 million in profits. But wait, we're far from finished.

There was the rent Jason had to pay for the use of his 10 store locations; then there were those pesky employees who for some reason expected to get paid for selling gum and keeping the stores clean and running smoothly; there were electricity and heating costs, trash removal, and accounting and all kinds of administrative costs (so Jason could keep track of all the money and gum flying all over the place)—and that stuff adds up. In this case, another $2 million in expenses to be exact. That got Jason's business down to $2 million in profits. But as you suspected, we're not done yet.

Jason's business had to pay taxes. The government needs money to provide services to its citizens, and profitable businesses must pay their share of taxes to keep it going. In the case of Jason's Gum Shops, that tax is equal to 40 percent of income (a fairly standard rate for many businesses). So 40 percent of the $2 million in profits that Jason's gum business earned last year had to go to the government in the form of taxes. Since 40 percent of $2 million is $800,000, that left Jason's Gum Shops with a *net profit* of $1.2 million.

Actually, Jason provided us with all that information about last year's income in a very neat table, known as an *income statement* (see Table 3.1).

So there you have it. Jason's Gum Shops earned $1.2 million last year. Jason thinks that makes the business worth a total of $12 million. He is willing to sell us a piece of that business, in any size up to half the entire business,

**TABLE 3.1   Jason's Gum Shops Annual Income Statement (For the Last 12 Months)**

| | |
|---|---|
| Total sales | $10,000,000 |
| Cost of goods sold | |
| (i.e., the gum) | −6,000,000 |
| Gross profit | 4,000,000 |
| | |
| Selling, general, & | |
| administrative expenses | −2,000,000 |
| | |
| Income before taxes | 2,000,000 |
| Taxes (@40%) | −800,000 |
| | |
| Net income | $1,200,000 |

at that $12 million valuation (i.e., $6 million for half, $1.2 million for a 10 percent stake, $120,000 for 1 percent ownership, and one share equaling one-millionth of the business for a measly $12). Should we do it? To keep it simple, let's take a look at what we'll be getting for each $12 share.

Well, Jason has divided his business into 1 million equal shares. That means, if the whole business earned $1,200,000, each share earned one-millionth of that amount. Since $1,200,000 divided by 1,000,000 is $1.20, each $12 share was entitled to $1.20 in earnings. Is that a good deal? Let's look at it this way. If we invest $12 for a piece of Jason's business and it earns us $1.20 in the first year, our first-year return on our investment would be

$$\$1.20/\$12, \text{ or } 10\%$$

A 10 percent return in our first year! Pretty darn good, right? In Chapter 2 we discussed that, at the very least, we had to beat the 6 percent annual return from a 10-year U.S. government bond. That's because buying those bonds would earn us 6 percent without having to take *any* risk. Since earning 10 percent is clearly more than earning 6 percent, ipso fatso, is it then true that paying $12 for a share that earns $1.20 a good deal?

Well, life isn't quite that simple (but as we'll see in a later chapter, almost!). The bottom line is—we're off to a great start, but we have to consider a few more things before we can make up our mind.

First, $1.20 per share is what Jason's Gum Shops earned *last* year. We have to determine whether we think the business will earn that $1.20 in the coming year—or *more* than that—or maybe *less*. Last year's earnings may be a good starting point for estimating next year's earnings, but it may not. If Jason's Gum Shops doesn't earn $1.20 next year, the business won't be earning that 10 percent we expected on the $12 per share we just paid—it could be higher—but it could be lower.

Second, once we come up with our estimate for how much Jason's business will earn next year, we have to determine how *confident* we are in our prediction. If we're taking a wild guess because we have no idea whether gum sales are steady from year to year, whether Jason's gum stores are just a fad, or whether new competition from other candy stores will affect Jason's profits, then our estimate may be suspect. But we have to be reasonable. If we're not sure whether earnings will be $1.50 or $2.00 per share, that kind of uncertainty is fine. Both of those numbers will represent that Jason's business is earning more than that 10 percent on our initial $12-per-share cost. On the other hand, if we're uncertain whether the earnings will be 20 cents per share or $1.20, then our guaranteed 6 percent from the government bond may start to look a whole lot better.

The third little detail we haven't yet considered is that next year is only one year. Even if Jason's Gum Shops earns $1.20 *next* year (or a lot more or a lot less), what about all the years after that? Will earnings keep growing every year? Maybe each store will keep selling more gum each year, and earnings will increase that way. Or maybe if 10 stores can make $1.20 per share, getting to 20 stores in a few years will cause earnings to grow to $2.40 per share or even higher? Of course, the gum business could always turn sour (sorry) in the next few years, causing gum earnings to remain stuck at levels well below $1.20 for a long time. And there's more . . .

Okay, you're beginning to panic. I can feel it. This stuff is too hard. How are you going to figure it all out? How can anyone? And even if you take your best shot, am I expecting you (and my kids, for that matter) to "gamble" *real* money on a pile of guesses and estimates? And, oh yeah, aren't there tons of MBAs, PhDs, smart financial types, and professional investment analysts, not to mention full-time money managers, trying to figure out pretty much the same things? How can little old *you* compete with all those hardworking, smart, sophisticated guys?

All right already, enough, calm down. Sheesh, can't I take you anywhere? Have a little faith. Hang in there. I'll do that summary thing, tell you what's important to remember, and we'll move on. Man, if I have to hold your hand for every little thing . . .

*So, here's what you need to know:*

1. Buying a *share* in a business means you are purchasing a portion (or percentage interest) of that business. You are then entitled to a portion of that business's future earnings.

2. Figuring out what a business is worth involves estimating (okay, guessing) how much the business will earn in the future.

3. The earnings from your share of the profits must give you more money than you would receive by placing that same amount of money in a risk-free 10-year U.S. government bond. (Remember: Last chapter we set 6 percent as your absolute minimum annual return when government bond rates fall below 6 percent) and

4. No, I haven't forgotten about the *magic formula*. But you're going to have to stop bugging me about it, okay? Sheesh!

# Chapter Four

GREAT, FIGURING OUT WHAT A BUSINESS is worth isn't easy. After lots of guessing and estimating, maybe you get it right and maybe you get it wrong. But what if you could? What if you could figure out what a business was really worth? Is there something you could do with that information? Is there really a place like I promised in the first chapter, a place where you can buy a business for half its true value? A place where you can get $1,000 of value for only $500? You bet there is. But first, let's spend a few minutes in business school.

For the past nine years, I have taught an investing course to a group of graduate business students at an Ivy League university. Needless to say, this is a pretty smart group of students. Each year, on the first day of class, I walk in and open the newspaper to the financial section. Found there are pages and pages of tables with lots of numbers in tiny print. (Sounds great so far, right?) Anyway, posted in these tables is a list of company names, and next to each name is a bunch of prices.

"Call out the name of a big, well-known company," I say. The students come up with companies like General Electric, IBM, General Motors, and Abercrombie & Fitch. Actually, it doesn't really matter what companies the students shout out. My main point is so easy to make, any company name in almost any industry, large or small, well-known or not, will do. The result is always the same.

I look in the paper next to General Electric and read off the numbers. "It says here that the price for one share of General Electric was $35 yesterday. It also says here that the highest price that General Electric shares have sold for over the last year was $53 per share. The lowest price for a share over the last year was $29.

"For IBM, it's the same thing. You could have purchased one share of IBM yesterday for $85. Over the past year, shares of IBM have sold for as much as $93 and for as little as $55.

"General Motors sold for $37 per share yesterday. But over the last year, shares have sold for between $30 and $68. For Abercrombie & Fitch, which was selling for $27 per share yesterday, the range of prices per share over the last year has been between $15 per share at the lowest and just over $33 per share for a high price."

I then point out that that's a pretty wide range of prices for shares and a pretty short period of time for them to change so much. Looking at the price for shares over a two- to three-year period would give us an even wider range.

So here's the question that I always ask: How can this be? These are big, well-known companies. Each of these companies has divided its ownership into millions (and sometimes billions) of equal shares, just like Jason did with his gum shops. Initially, companies sell their shares to the public (to both individuals and big institutional investors). After that, though, the people who buy these shares are free to sell them to anyone they want.

Each day the newspaper lists the names of thousands of companies and the price at which people have been buying and selling an ownership share in each. The *trading* back and forth of these ownership shares takes place in a number of locations and over computer networks. These ownership shares are referred to as shares of *stock,* and collectively, this buying and selling activity is referred to as the *stock market.*

A company as large as IBM or General Motors might have divided its ownership stake into something like a billion equal shares. That means that if at one point during the year you can purchase one share of General Motors for $30 (and for our example we assume the ownership of General Motors has been divided into 1 billion equal pieces, or shares), then the implied price to purchase the entire company (all 1 billion shares) would be $30 billion. However, if at some point during the same year, General Motors shares could have been purchased for $60 each, that would indicate that the cost to purchase all of General Motors would be $60 billion.

So I ask the question again: How can this be? Can the value of General Motors, the largest car manufacturer in North America, change that much within the same year? Can a company that large be worth $30 billion one day and then a few months later be worth $60 billion? Are they selling twice as many cars, making twice as much money, or doing something drastically different in their business to justify such a large change in value? Of course, it's possible. But what about the big price changes in IBM, Abercrombie & Fitch, and General Electric? Does something happen each and every year to account for large changes in the value of most companies?

Remember, every year the results are the same. For pretty much any company that my students name, the range of high and low prices, over the course of only one year, is huge. Does this make sense? Well, to save the class time (and since my attention span is usually a matter of seconds), I usually blurt out the answer. *No!* It makes no sense that the *values* of most companies swing wildly from high to low, or low to high, during the course of each and every year. On the other hand, it seems pretty clear that the *prices* of the shares in most companies swing around wildly each and every year. All you have to do is look in the newspaper to see that that's true.

So I ask my room full of smart, sophisticated students to try to explain why. Why do the *prices* of all these businesses move around so much each year if the *values* of their businesses can't possibly change that much? Well, it's a good question, so I generally let my students spend some time offering up complicated explanations and theories.

In fact, it's such a good question that professors have developed whole fields of economic, mathematical, and social study to try to explain it. Even more incredible, most of this academic work has involved coming up with theories as to why something that clearly makes no sense, actually makes sense. You have to be *really* smart to do that.

So why do share prices move around so much every year when it seems clear that the values of the underlying businesses do not? Well, here's how I explain it to my students: Who knows and who cares?

Maybe people go nuts a lot. Maybe it's hard to predict future earnings. Maybe it's hard to decide what a *fair* rate of return on your purchase price is. Maybe people get a little depressed sometimes and don't want to pay a lot for stuff. Maybe people get excited sometimes and are willing to pay a lot. So maybe people simply justify high prices by making high estimates for future earnings when they are happy and justify low prices by making low estimates when they are sad.

But like I said, maybe people just go nuts a lot (still my favorite). The truth is that I don't really have to know *why* people are willing to buy and sell shares of most companies at wildly different prices over very short periods of time. I just have to know that *they do*! Why is this helpful? Let's think about that.

Suppose you figured that a business (perhaps one like Jason's Gum Shops) was worth between $10 and $12 per share, and at varying times during the year, its shares could be purchased for between $6 and $11. Well, if you were confident about your estimate of what the business was worth, then deciding whether to buy shares when they were trading near $11 might be a difficult decision. But when shares in that same company during that same year were available at close to $6, your decision might well become much easier! At $6 per share, if your estimates of value were close to correct, then you would be buying shares in Jason's Gum Shops for only 50 or 60 cents on the dollar (for 50 or 60 percent of what they were truly worth).

One of the greatest stock market writers and thinkers, Benjamin Graham, put it this way. Imagine that you are partners in the ownership of a business with a crazy guy named Mr. Market. Mr. Market is subject to wild mood swings. Each day he offers to buy your share of the business or sell you his share of the business at a particular price. Mr. Market always leaves the decision completely to you, and every day you have three choices. You can sell your shares to Mr. Market at his stated price, you can buy Mr. Market's shares at that same price, or you can do nothing.

Sometimes Mr. Market is in such a good mood that he names a price that is much higher than the true worth of the business. On those days, it would probably make sense for you to sell Mr. Market your share of the business. On other days, he is in such a poor mood that he names a very low price for the business. On those days, you might want to take advantage of Mr. Market's crazy offer to sell you shares at such a low price and to buy Mr. Market's share of the business. If the price named by Mr. Market is neither very high nor extraordinarily low relative to the value of the business, you might very logically choose to do nothing.

In the world of the stock market, that's exactly how it works. The stock market is Mr. Market! If, according to the daily newspaper, General Motors is selling for $37 per share, you have three choices: You can buy shares in General Motors for $37 each, you can sell your shares in General Motors and receive $37 each, or you can do nothing. If you think GM is really worth $70 per share, then you might consider $37 a ridiculously low price and decide to buy some shares. If you think GM is really worth only $30 or $35 per share (and you happen to own some shares), you might decide to sell to "Mr. Market" at $37. If you think each share of General Motors is worth between $40 and $45 per share, you may decide to do nothing. At $37 per share, the price is not at a big enough discount for you to buy, nor is $37 a generous enough offer to make you want to sell.

In short, you are never required to act. *You* alone can choose to act only when the price offered by Mr. Market appears very low (when you might decide to buy some shares) or extremely high (when you might consider selling any shares you own to Mr. Market).

Graham referred to this practice of buying shares of a company only when they trade at a large discount to true value as investing with a *margin of safety*. The difference between your estimated value per share of, say, $70 and the purchase price of your shares of perhaps $37 would represent a margin of safety for your investment. If your original calculations of the value of shares in a company like General Motors were too high or the car business unexpectedly took a turn for the worse after your purchase, the margin of safety in your original purchase price could still protect you from losing money.

Even if you originally estimated fair value to be $70, and it turned out that $60 or even $50 was closer to the true value for each share, a purchase price of $37 would leave enough margin for you to still make money on your original investment! Graham figured that always using the margin of safety principle when deciding whether to purchase shares of a business from a crazy partner like Mr. Market was the secret to making safe and reliable investment profits. In fact, these two concepts—requiring a margin of safety for your investment purchases and viewing the stock market as if it were a partner like Mr. Market—have been used with much success by some of the greatest investors of all time.

But wait! There's still a problem here. Okay, maybe a few. First, as we discussed, how are you supposed to know what a business is worth? If you can't place a fair value on a company, then you can't divide that number by the number of shares that exist, and you can't figure out what the fair value of a share of stock is. So even if a share of General Motors sells for $30 on one day and $60 per share a few months later, you have no idea whether one of those prices is cheap and one is expensive or both are cheap or both expensive, or whatever! In short, from what we've learned so far, you wouldn't know a bargain price if it hit you in the head!

Second, if you could figure out a fair price or price range for the business, how would you know whether you were right, or even close to right? Remember, in the process of figuring out the value of a business, all you do is make a bunch of guesses and estimates. Those estimates involve predicting earnings for a business for many years into the future. Even experts (whatever that means) have a tough time doing that.

Third, as we already covered, aren't there tons of smart, hardworking people trying to figure out all this stuff, too? Aren't there lots of stock market analysts and professional investors who spend their time trying to figure out what companies are really worth? Even if I could really teach *you* how to invest, wouldn't these smart, knowledgeable, and experienced people be better at it than you? Wouldn't these people scoop up all of the obvious bargains before you got there? How can you compete with those guys? All you did was buy a book—a book that says even kids (okay, teenagers) can learn how to make *big* money in the stock market. Does that make sense? What chance do you really have?

Well, a sane person might start to feel a little foolish about now. But you paid good money for this book! You could already be a few cards short of a full deck. So at least we've got that going for us! In any case, ready or not, here comes the summary:

1. Stock *prices* move around wildly over very short periods of time. This does not mean that the *values* of the underlying companies have changed very much during that same period. In effect, the stock market acts very much like a crazy guy named Mr. Market.

2. It is a good idea to buy shares of a company at a big discount to your estimated value of those shares. Buying shares at a large discount to value will provide you with a large *margin of safety* and lead to safe and consistently profitable investments.

3. From what we've learned so far, you wouldn't know a bargain-priced stock if it hit you in the head.

4. Being a few cards short of a full deck, you might as well keep reading.

# Chapter Five

I LOVE MOVIES, and *The Karate Kid* is one of my favorites. Of course, I would like any art form where eating popcorn and candy are part of the deal. But there is one scene in this particular movie that holds special meaning for me. In it, the old karate master, Mr. Miyagi, is supposed to be teaching his teenage apprentice, Daniel, how to fight. The boy is new at school and being bullied by a group of karate-trained toughs. Daniel hopes learning karate will help him stand up to his tormentors and win the girl of his dreams. But instead of teaching him karate, Mr. Miyagi puts Daniel to work—waxing cars, painting fences, and sanding floors.

So after a whirlwind of scenes showing poor Daniel working his fingers to the bone—waxing, painting, and sanding—the youth has finally had enough. He confronts Mr. Miyagi and essentially says, "Why am I wasting my time doing these simple and menial tasks when I should be learning karate?" Mr. Miyagi has Daniel stand up from his sanding duties and starts throwing jabs at the young boy while yelling "Wax on! Wax off!" Daniel deflects each jab with the swirling motions he learned from so many hours waxing cars. Next, Mr. Miyagi throws a punch while yelling "Paint the fence." Once again, Daniel deflects the punch, this time using the up-and-down action of painting a fence. Similarly, Mr. Miyagi's karate kick is then stopped by Daniel's expert floor-sanding ability.

In effect, by learning these few simple techniques, Daniel has unwittingly become a karate master. Now in good movies, the viewer participates in something called the *willing suspension of disbelief*. In other words, we kind of know that Ralph Macchio, the actor who plays Daniel in the movie, couldn't really use that waxing thing to defend himself in a dark alley. In the real world, before he could finish his first coat, Mr. Macchio would probably get smacked in the head and drop like a sack of potatoes. But while caught up in a movie, we're ready and more than willing to believe that Mr. Miyagi's simple methods can truly work wonders.

Well, I'm going to have to ask you to do a little suspending of disbelief, too. Not because what you're going to learn doesn't make sense. On the contrary, the two concepts in this chapter are simple and obvious. It's just that these two concepts are so very basic, you'll have a hard time believing that such simple tools can turn *you* into a stock market master. But pay close attention now, and I promise you won't get a smack in the head later.

When we last left Jason, the hero of our story, he had just asked us to chew over an exciting proposal. His proposal was simple: Would we want to buy a piece of his wildly successful chain of gum stores, Jason's Gum Shops? (You want some, you know you want some . . .) But as much as Jason wanted to sell us a piece of his business, giving him an answer wasn't turning out to be so simple.

By looking at the *income statement* that Jason had provided us, it turned out that Jason's chain of 10 gum shops had earned a total of $1.2 million last year—pretty impressive. Since Jason had divided his business into 1 million equal shares, we had concluded that each share was therefore entitled to $1.20 in earnings ($1,200,000 divided by 1,000,000 shares). At Jason's asking price of $12 for each share, that meant that based on last year's earnings, Jason's Gum Shops would have given us a 10 percent return for each $12 share purchased ($1.20 divided by $12 = 10 percent).

That 10 percent return, calculated by dividing the earnings per share for the year by the share price, is known as the *earnings yield*. We then compared the earnings yield of 10 percent we could receive from an investment in Jason's business with the 6 percent return we could earn risk free from investing in a 10-year U.S. government bond. We concluded, without too much trouble, that earning 10 percent per year on our investment was better than earning 6 percent. Of course, although that analysis was simple, we identified a bunch of problems.

First, Jason's Gum Shops earned that $1.20 per share last year. Next year's earnings might turn out to be a completely different story. If Jason's business earned less than $1.20 next year, we wouldn't earn a 10 percent return on our investment and maybe we would be better off with a sure 6 percent from the government bond. Second, even if Jason's business did earn the $1.20 per share next year, or even more, that's only one year. How do we know, or how would we ever know, how much Jason's Gum Shops would earn in future years? It could be a lot more than $1.20 per share, but it could be a lot less, and our earnings yield could drop significantly below the 6 percent we could have earned risk free from the U.S. government. Lastly, even if we had an opinion about future earnings, how could we ever have any confidence that our predictions would turn out to be right?

In short, all of our problems seem to boil down to this: It's hard to predict the future. If we can't predict the future earnings of a business, then it's hard to place a value on that business. If we can't value a business, then even if Mr. Market goes crazy sometimes and offers us unbelievable bargain prices, we won't recognize them. But rather than focusing on all the things that we don't know, let's go over a couple of the things that we do know.

As we discussed, Jason's Gum Shops earned $1.20 per share last year. At a price of $12 per share, our earnings yield was therefore $1.20 divided by $12, or 10 percent—easy enough. But what if Jason's Gum Shops earned $2.40 per share last year? What if we could still buy a share for $12? What would the earnings yield be then? Well, $2.40 divided by $12 equals 20 percent. Therefore, if Jason's Gum Shops had earned $2.40 per share last year, at a price of $12 per share, the earnings yield would be 20 percent. If Jason's Gum Shops had earned $3.60 per share last year, at a price of $12 per share, the earnings yield would be 30 percent! But it gets easier.

Now follow closely because there are only two main points in this chapter and here comes the question that will determine whether you understand the first. All things being equal, if you could buy a share of Jason's Gum Shops for $12, which of those earnings results would you prefer? Would you prefer that Jason's Gum

Shops had earned $1.20 per share last year, $2.40 per share last year, or $3.60 per share last year? In other words, would you prefer that the earnings yield calculated using last year's earnings was 10 percent, 20 percent, or 30 percent? Drumroll, please. If you answered that 30 percent is obviously better than 20 percent and 10 percent, you would be correct! And that's the point—you would rather have a higher earnings yield than a lower one; you would rather the business earn more relative to the price you are paying than less! Wax on!

Now that wasn't so hard, but here comes the second point of the chapter, which focuses on something a bit different from the first (otherwise, I would be saying the same thing twice, which would be wasting your time, which is something I would never do unless I put it in parentheses). The first point related to *price*—how much we receive in earnings relative to our purchase price. In other words, is the purchase price a bargain or not? But beyond price, we might also want to know something about the nature of the business itself. In short, are we buying a *good* business or a *bad* business?

Of course, there are plenty of ways we could define what makes a business either good or bad. Among other things, we could look at the quality of its products or services, the loyalty of its customers, the value of its brands, the efficiency of its operations, the talent of its management, the strength of its competitors, or the long-term prospects of its business. Obviously, any of these criteria, either alone or in combination, would be helpful in evaluating whether we were purchasing a good or a bad business. All of these assessments would also involve making guesses, estimates, and/or predictions. As we already agreed, that's a pretty hard thing to do.

So once again it might make sense to first examine some things that we already know. In fact, let's not make *any* predictions at all. Instead, let's just look at what happened *last* year. For instance, what if we found out that it cost Jason $400,000 to build each of his gum stores (including inventory, store displays, etc.) and that each of those stores earned him $200,000 last year. That would mean, at least based on last year's results, that a typical store in the Jason's Gum Shops chain earns $200,000 each year from an initial investment of only $400,000. This works out to a 50 percent yearly return ($200,000 divided by $400,000) on the initial cost of opening a gum store. This result is often referred to as a 50 percent *return on capital*. Without knowing much else, earning $200,000 each year from a store that costs $400,000 to build sounds like a pretty good business. But here comes the hard part (not really).

What if Jason had a friend, Jimbo, who also owned a chain of stores? What if you had a chance to buy a piece of Jimbo's store chain, Just Broccoli? What if it also cost Jimbo $400,000 to open a new store? But what if each of those stores earned only $10,000 last year? Earning $10,000 a year from a store that costs you $400,000 to build works out to a one-year return of only 2.5 percent, or a 2.5 percent return on capital. So here's the tough question: Which business sounds better? Jason's Gum Shops, a business where each store earned $200,000 last year and cost $400,000 to build, or Just Broccoli, a business where each store earned $10,000 last year but also cost $400,000 to build? In other words, which sounds better—a business that earns a 50 percent return on capital or one that earns a 2.5 percent return on capital? Of course, the answer is obvious—and that's the second point! You would rather own a business that earns a high return on capital than one that earns a low return on capital! Wax off (or paint the fence or sand something or whatever)!*

But here comes the big finish. Remember how I told you this chapter was going to be hard to believe? That by using just two simple tools you could actually become a "stock market master"? Well, believe it. *You* are a stock market master.

---

*To find out what Jimbo should do, check out the box at the end of the chapter!

How? Well, as you'll see next chapter, it turns out that *if you just stick to buying* good *companies (ones that have a high return on capital) and to buying those companies only at* bargain prices *(at prices that give you a high earnings yield), you can end up systematically buying many of the good companies that crazy Mr. Market has decided to literally give away.* You can achieve investment returns that beat the pants off even the best investment professionals (including the smartest professional I know). You can beat the returns of top-notch professors and outperform every academic study ever done. In fact, you can more than double the annual returns of the stock market averages!

But there's more. You can do it all by yourself. You can do it with low risk. You can do it without making any predictions. You can do it by following a simple formula that uses only the two basic concepts you just learned in this chapter. You can do it for the rest of your life—*and* you can choose to do it only after you are convinced that it really works.

Hard to believe? Well, it's my job to prove it. Your job is to take the time to read and understand that the only reason this simple method actually works is that it makes perfect sense! But first, as always, here comes the summary:

1. Paying a *bargain price* when you purchase a share in a business is a good thing. One way to do this is to

purchase a business that earns more relative to the price you are paying rather than less. In other words, a higher *earnings yield* is better than a lower one.

2. Buying a share of a *good* business is better than buying a share of a *bad* business. One way to do this is to purchase a business that can invest its own money at high rates of return rather than purchasing a business that can only invest at lower ones. In other words, businesses that earn a high *return on capital* are better than businesses that earn a low return on capital.

3. Combining points 1 and 2, buying *good* businesses at *bargain* prices is the secret to making lots of money.

And most important,

4. Don't give money to guys named Jimbo.

In fact, unless Jimbo expects those Just Broccoli stores to earn a lot more in the coming years (a presumption that would obviously involve making predictions about the future), it seems pretty clear that Jimbo's business is so bad he shouldn't even be building Just Broccoli stores. If he has a choice of building a new store for $400,000 that will earn him just 2.5 percent each year on his investment or buying a U.S. government bond that will earn him 6 percent on his investment—risk free—what's the point of even building a store in the first place? By opening Just Broccoli stores, Jimbo is actually throwing money away! (Even though it looks like he is earning 2.5 percent on his investment in a new store, in reality he is throwing away the added 3.5 percent he could earn by simply buying a risk-free U.S. government bond!)

# Chapter Six

So WE'RE READY FOR the *magic formula*! Of course, you're still probably thinking it won't work or it'll be too hard or there's something wrong with a book that even claims to have a magic formula. But if it makes you feel any better, even the great Benjamin Graham, one of the most respected and influential pioneers in the investment field, the man who introduced us to the concepts of Mr. Market and margin of safety, wrote about and used a magic formula of his own. Okay, so he didn't really call it that (apparently, the man had some dignity). But Graham felt that most individual investors, and even many professional investors, would have a hard time making the type of predictions and performing the level of analysis necessary to value and invest in businesses on their own. Graham figured that by sharing a simple formula, one that made sense and had worked well in the past, individual investors would be able to achieve excellent investment results with a high degree of safety.

Graham's formula involved purchasing companies whose stock prices were so low that the purchase price was actually lower than the proceeds that would be received from simply shutting down the business and selling off the company's assets in a fire sale (he called these stocks by various names: *bargain issues, net-current-asset stocks,* or stocks selling below their *net liquidation value*). Graham stated that it seems "ridiculously simple to say" that if one could buy a group of 20 or 30 companies that were cheap enough to meet the strict requirements of his formula, without doing any further analysis, the *"results should be quite satisfactory."* In fact, Graham used this formula with much success for over 30 years.

Unfortunately, the formula was designed during a period when many stocks were priced cheaply. For several decades after the stock market crash of 1929 and the Great Depression that followed, investing in stocks was considered to be an extremely risky business. Investors, for the most part, were therefore unwilling to place a high value on stocks for fear of losing their money again. Although Graham's formula has continued to work over the years, especially during periods when stock prices are particularly depressed, in today's markets there are usually few, if any, stocks that meet the strict requirements of Graham's original formula.

But that's okay. By using his formula successfully for so many years, Graham showed that a simple system for finding obviously cheap stocks could lead to safe and consistently good investment returns. If Mr. Market was willing to sell him a group of stocks at prices so low that they met his formula's strict requirements, Graham figured that *on average* he would end up owning a basket of bargains. Sure, the low prices of some of the stocks would be justified. Some companies deserve low prices because their future prospects are poor. *But on average, Graham figured that the purchases made by using his formula would be bargains—bargains created by Mr. Market practically giving away businesses at unreasonably low prices.* Graham suggested that by buying a group of these bargain stocks, investors could safely earn a high return without worrying about a few bad purchases and without doing complicated analysis of individual stocks.

Of course, that leaves us with an obvious challenge. Can we come up with a new formula, one that can beat the market averages with low risk? Can we find one that not only works in today's market but one that is flexible enough to work far into the future—regardless of the overall level of the market? Well, as you might have guessed, we can. In fact, you already know what it is!

Last chapter we learned that, all things being equal, if we have the choice of buying a stock with a high earnings yield (one that earns a lot relative to the price we are paying) or buying one with a low earnings yield (one that earns very little relative to the price we are paying), we might as well choose the one with the high earnings yield. We also learned that, all things being equal, if the choice is between buying shares in a company that earns a high return on capital (a company whose stores or factories earn a lot relative to the cost to build them) and buying shares in a company that earns a low return on capital (a company whose stores or factories earn very little relative to the cost to build them, like Just Broccoli), we might as well choose the one with the high return on capital!

So here it comes. What do you think would happen if we simply decided to buy shares in companies that had *both* a high earnings yield and a high return on capital? In other words, *what would happen if we decided to only buy shares in good businesses (ones with high returns on capital) but only when they were available at bargain prices (priced to give us a high earnings yield)*? What would happen? Well, I'll tell you what would happen: *We would make a lot of money!* (Or as Graham might put it, "The profits would be *quite satisfactory!*")

But does it make sense that something this simple and obvious would actually work in the real world? Well, to answer that question, a logical first step might be to go back and see how a disciplined strategy of buying *good businesses at bargain prices* would have worked in the past. As it turns out, following a simple, commonsense investment strategy actually would have worked pretty well.

Over the last 17 years, owning a portfolio of approximately 30 stocks that had the best combination of a high return on capital and a high earnings yield would have returned approximately *30.8 percent* per year. Investing at that rate for 17 years, *$11,000 would have turned into well over $1 million.** Of course, for some people, that might not seem like such a great return. On the other hand, those people are basically nuts!

During those same 17 years, the overall market averaged a return of about *12.3 percent* per year. At that rate, *$11,000 would* still *have turned into an impressive $79,000.* While that's certainly a lot, *$1 million is more*! And you could have made that $1 million *while taking much less risk*

---

*The special database used for our magic formula study (Compustat's "Point in Time" database) contains data going back a total of 17 years. It contains the exact information known by Compustat customers at the time of each stock purchase. At a rate of 30.8 percent per year for 17 years, $11,000 would grow over 96× to $1,056,000 before taxes and transaction costs.

than investing in the overall market. But we'll talk more about that later.

For now, let's see just how the magic formula was put together. In that way, we can begin to understand why such a simple formula works and why it should continue to work far into the future. Later, we'll learn, in step-by-step fashion, how to apply the magic formula to find winning investments today. But keep in mind, the mechanics aren't the important part; the computer will be doing most of the work. As you read in Chapter 1, it will be your belief in the overwhelming logic of the magic formula that will make the formula work for you in the long run. So let's try to understand how the magic formula chooses good companies at bargain prices.

The formula starts with a list of the largest 3,500 companies available for trading on one of the major U.S. stock exchanges.* It then assigns a rank to those companies, from 1 to 3,500, based on their return on capital. The company whose business had the highest return on capital would be assigned a rank of 1, and the company with the lowest return on capital (probably a company actually losing money) would receive a rank of 3,500. Similarly, the company that had the 232nd best return on capital would be assigned a rank of 232.

*Details of this test are provided in the Appendix section (certain financial stocks and utilities are excluded from our stock universe).

Next, the formula follows the same procedure, but this time, the ranking is done using earnings yield. The company with the highest earnings yield is assigned a rank of 1, and the company with the lowest earnings yield receives a rank of 3,500. Likewise, the company with the 153rd highest earnings yield out of our list of 3,500 companies would be assigned a rank of 153.

Finally, the formula just combines the rankings. The formula isn't looking for the company that ranks best on return on capital or the one with the highest earnings yield. Rather, *the formula looks for the companies that have the best combination of those two factors.* So, a company that ranked 232nd best in return on capital and 153rd highest in earnings yield would receive a combined ranking of 385 (232 + 153). A company that ranked 1st in return on capital but only 1,150th best in earnings yield would receive a combined ranking of 1,151 (1,150 + 1).*

If you're not a numbers person, don't worry. Just keep in mind that the companies that receive the best combined rankings are the ones that have the best *combination* of both factors. In this system, the company that had the 232nd best return on capital could outrank the company that ranked 1st in return on capital. Why? Because we could purchase the company that had the

---

*The better combined ranking is, therefore, 385.

232nd best return on capital (an excellent ranking out of 3,500) for a price low enough to give us a very high earnings yield (153rd cheapest out of 3,500 based on earnings yield). Getting excellent rankings in both categories (though not the top-ranked in either) would be better under this ranking system than being the top-ranked in one category with only a pretty good ranking in the other.

Pretty simple, right? But it can't be *this* easy! Can a portfolio of 30 or so of the highest-ranked stocks really get such great investment results? Well, consider this. Take a look at the returns that would have been achieved over the last 17 years if we had simply followed the recommendations of the magic formula (see Table 6.1).

Oops! This can't be. The results are just too good! Surely, something *must* be wrong here. We'll really have to examine these results very closely. But let's say we leave that for the next chapter. For now, we can review the short summary and spend some more time enjoying the results from using the magic formula. They appear to be *quite satisfactory.*

## Quick Summary

1. Ben Graham had a "magic formula." Graham figured that purchases that could meet the strict

**TABLE 6.1   Magic Formula Results**

|  | Magic Formula | Market Average* | S&P 500 |
|---|---|---|---|
| 1988 | 27.1% | 24.8% | 16.6% |
| 1989 | 44.6 | 18.0 | 31.7 |
| 1990 | 1.7 | (16.1) | (3.1) |
| 1991 | 70.6 | 45.6 | 30.5 |
| 1992 | 32.4 | 11.4 | 7.6 |
| 1993 | 17.2 | 15.9 | 10.1 |
| 1994 | 22.0 | (4.5) | 1.3 |
| 1995 | 34.0 | 29.1 | 37.6 |
| 1996 | 17.3 | 14.9 | 23.0 |
| 1997 | 40.4 | 16.8 | 33.4 |
| 1998 | 25.5 | (2.0) | 28.6 |
| 1999 | 53.0 | 36.1 | 21.0 |
| 2000 | 7.9 | (16.8) | (9.1) |
| 2001 | 69.6 | 11.5 | (11.9) |
| 2002 | (4.0) | (24.2) | (22.1) |
| 2003 | 79.9 | 68.8 | 28.7 |
| 2004 | 19.3 | 17.8 | 10.9 |
|  | **30.8%** | **12.3%** | **12.4%** |

*Note: The "market average" return is an *equally weighted* index of our 3,500-stock universe. Each stock in the index contributes equally to the return. The S&P 500 index is a *market-weighted* index of 500 large stocks. Larger stocks (those with the highest market capitalizations) are counted more heavily than smaller stocks.

requirements of his formula were likely to be, on average, bargains—bargains created by Mr. Market's practically giving away businesses at unreasonably low prices.

2. Today, few companies meet the strict requirements outlined by Graham.

3. We have designed a new magic formula—a formula that seeks to *find good companies at bargain prices*.

4. The new formula appears to work. In fact, it appears to work too well.

5. Before piling every penny we have into the magic formula, we should probably examine the results more closely.

# Chapter Seven

"IT AIN'T THE THINGS WE DON'T KNOW that get us in trouble," said Artemus Ward, a nineteenth-century newspaper columnist. "It's the things we *know* that ain't so." And that, in a nutshell, is our problem. The magic formula looks like it works. In fact, the results are so good there can hardly be any argument. And of course, we want it to work. Who wouldn't want to make lots of money without trying all that hard? But does the magic formula *really* work? Sure, all the numbers look good, but do we know where they came from (or who they've been with, for that matter)? More important, do we know where they're going? Even if the formula worked in the past, are we merely learning how to "fight the *last* war"? Will the formula continue to work in the future?

Good questions, certainly. Before what we learned from last chapter gets us into too much trouble, let's see if we can find some good answers.

First up, where *did* all those numbers come from? There's often a problem when looking back and making assumptions about what could have been accomplished in the past. While a computer stock-picking formula may appear to have generated spectacular theoretical returns, duplicating those results in the real world may be quite difficult. For instance, the magic formula may be picking companies that are so small that few people can really buy them. Often, small companies have very few shares available for purchase, and even a small amount of demand for those shares can push share prices higher. If that's the case, the formula may look great on paper, but in the real world, the fantastic results can't be replicated. That's why it's important that the companies chosen by the magic formula be pretty large.

Last chapter, the magic formula ranked 3,500 of the largest companies available for trading on the major U.S. stock exchanges. The formula then chose its favorite stocks from that group. Even the very smallest of those 3,500 companies still had a market value (the number of shares times the stock price) of over $50 million.* With

*See Appendix section for details.

companies of that size, individual investors should be able to buy a reasonable number of shares without pushing prices higher.

But let's see what happens when we raise the bar a little bit. It would certainly be nice if the magic formula worked for companies whether they were large or small. That way we could be more confident that the basic principle of buying good companies at bargain prices works for companies of any size. So instead of choosing from the largest 3,500 companies, let's look at just the largest 2,500 companies. The smallest companies in this group have a market value of at least $200 million.

Over the last 17 years (ending in December 2004), the magic formula worked remarkably well for this group of larger companies, too. Owning a portfolio of 30 stocks chosen by the magic formula would have achieved an annual return of 23.7 percent. During the same period, the market's average return for this group was 12.4 percent per year. In other words, the magic formula practically doubled the market's average annual return.

But what if we take it one step further? Let's look back and see what happened when we narrowed the group to just the largest 1,000 stocks—only the companies with market values over $1 billion. Even large institutional investors like mutual funds and large pension funds can buy these stocks. Well, take a look at this! (See Table 7.1.)

**TABLE 7.1 Magic Formula Results (Largest 1000 Stocks)**

|      | Magic Formula | Market Average* | S&P 500 |
|------|---------------|-----------------|---------|
| 1988 | 29.4%         | 19.6%           | 16.6%   |
| 1989 | 30.0          | 27.6            | 31.7    |
| 1990 | (6.0)         | (7.1)           | (3.1)   |
| 1991 | 51.5          | 34.4            | 30.5    |
| 1992 | 16.4          | 10.3            | 7.6     |
| 1993 | 0.5           | 14.4            | 10.1    |
| 1994 | 15.3          | 0.5             | 1.3     |
| 1995 | 55.9          | 31.4            | 37.6    |
| 1996 | 37.4          | 16.2            | 23.0    |
| 1997 | 41.0          | 19.6            | 33.4    |
| 1998 | 32.6          | 9.9             | 28.6    |
| 1999 | 14.4          | 35.1            | 21.0    |
| 2000 | 12.8          | (14.5)          | (9.1)   |
| 2001 | 38.2          | (9.2)           | (11.9)  |
| 2002 | (25.3)        | (22.7)          | (22.1)  |
| 2003 | 50.5          | 41.4            | 28.7    |
| 2004 | 27.6          | 17.3            | 10.9    |
|      | **22.9%**     | **11.7%**       | **12.4%** |

*Note: The "market average" return is an *equally weighted* average of our 1,000-stock universe. The S&P 500 index is a *market-weighted* index of 500 large stocks.

Once again, it appears that even the largest investors can practically double the market's compounded annual return simply by following the magic formula! But this can't be. There must be a catch. It just looks too darn easy! And of course, there *may* still be some problems. It's just that the problem of a magic formula that works only on paper but not in the real world isn't one of them.

Okay. So, the companies chosen by the magic formula aren't too small for investors to buy. But how about this? Maybe the magic formula just got lucky with a few good stock picks and that's why the whole average looks so good? If the magic formula doesn't stay lucky, relying on past results could be very dangerous. Fortunately, it's very unlikely that luck was much of a factor at all.

Throughout the 17 years of our study, we held a portfolio of roughly 30 stocks. Each stock selection was held for a period of one year.* In all, over 1,500 different stock picks were made for *each* of the tests (largest 3,500 stocks, largest 2,500 stocks, and largest 1,000 stocks). When we combine all of our tests, they are the results of over 4,500 separate magic formula selections! So it would be very difficult to argue that luck was a major factor. But there *must* be some other problem, right?

---

*See the Appendix section for more details.

How about this? While it's pretty nice that the magic formula can find 30 good companies that Mr. Market has decided to "throw away" at bargain prices, what if it can't? What if those few bargain opportunities were to disappear for some reason? What if Mr. Market simply wised up a bit and stopped offering us those few incredible bargains? If that happened, we really *would* be out of luck. So let's try a little experiment.

Starting with the largest 2,500 companies, what if we ranked them again using the magic formula? In other words, what if we ranked them from 1 to 2,500, from best to worst? Remember, the formula is looking for companies that have the best combination of a high return on capital and a high earnings yield. So the companies that appeared to be in good businesses and available at bargain prices would be ranked closer to number 1, while the companies losing lots of money that were offered at expensive prices would be ranked closer to 2,500.

Now what if we divided those 2,500 companies into 10 equal groups based on their rankings? In other words, Group 1 would contain the 250 companies that the magic formula viewed as good companies at bargain prices, Group 2 would be the second-highest-ranked group of 250 companies, Group 3 would be the third-highest-ranked group, and so on. Group 10, therefore, would be a group of 250 stocks that the magic formula ranked as being poor companies at expensive prices.

So what would happen if we did this every month for 17 years? What if we held each of those stock portfolios (each containing roughly 250 stocks) for one year and calculated the returns? Well, take a look (see Table 7.2).

Gee, that's interesting. The magic formula doesn't just work for only 30 stocks. The magic formula appears to work *in order*. The best-ranked stocks perform the best and as the ranking drops, so do the returns! Group 1 beats Group 2, Group 2 beats Group 3, Group 3 beats Group 4, and so on, straight down the line from Group 1 to Group 10. Group 1, our best-ranked stocks, beats Group 10, our worst-ranked stocks, by over 15 percent a year. That's pretty amazing!

**TABLE 7.2   Annualized Return (1988–2004)**

| | |
|---|---|
| Group 1 | 17.9% |
| Group 2 | 15.6 |
| Group 3 | 14.8 |
| Group 4 | 14.2 |
| Group 5 | 14.1 |
| Group 6 | 12.7 |
| Group 7 | 11.3 |
| Group 8 | 10.1 |
| Group 9 | 5.2 |
| Group 10 | 2.5 |

In fact, it appears as though the magic formula can predict the future! If we know how a group of companies is ranked by the magic formula, we have a pretty good idea of how well that group will perform on average as an investment in the future. That also means that if we can't, for some reason, buy the top 30 stocks as ranked by the magic formula, it's no big deal. Buying the next 30 should work pretty well also. So should the next 30! In fact, the whole group of top-ranked stocks appears to do well.

That may also solve one of our other potential problems. Remember how Ben Graham had his own "magic formula"? Buying a group of stocks that could meet the strict requirements of Graham's formula was a great way to make money. Unfortunately, in today's market, few, if any, companies qualify for purchase under Graham's original formula. That means Graham's formula isn't as useful as it once was. Fortunately, our magic formula doesn't seem to have that problem. It is merely a ranking formula. By definition, there always have to be stocks that rank at the top. Not only that, because the formula appears to work in order, we're not limited to just the top 30 stocks. Since the entire group of top-ranked stocks does well, there should always be plenty of high-performing stocks to choose from!

For those of you keeping score on the sidelines, it's looking pretty good for the magic formula. Come on.

That "ranking stocks in order" thing—man, that's pretty scary. It's been nice arguing back and forth about whether the magic formula *really* works, but the winner of that battle is pretty obvious. Maybe we should just stop the fight right now before somebody gets hurt?

Alas. Not so fast. Sure, the evidence is pretty convincing. But all that means is that the magic formula has worked in the past. How do we know the magic formula will continue to work in the future? After all, with me being such a blabbermouth, why won't everyone start using it? Won't that ruin everything?

Well, after we look at the summary, let's see . . .

1. The magic formula works for companies both large and small.
2. The magic formula was extensively tested. The great returns do not appear to be a matter of luck.
3. The magic formula ranks stocks *in order*. As a result, there should always be plenty of highly ranked stocks to choose from. The magic formula has been an incredibly accurate indicator of how a group of stocks will perform in the future!
4. Next chapter, we'll have to discuss whether the magic formula can continue to get such great results. (That would be nice!)

# Chapter Eight

I ADMIT IT. My knowledge of history is a little fuzzy.* I guess I should have listened better in class. But there's one part of our history that has always baffled me. I never really understood how we won the Revolutionary War. Here we were, these 13 little colonies, up against the strongest country in the world. England had the best navy, the mightiest army, the most money, and yet our scrappy little ragtag group of soldiers pulled out a victory! How'd that happen? Well, I have a theory. Given my limited knowledge, I don't know whether my theory has been

*Though my knowledge of Bob Newhart's old comedy routines is quite good.

extensively studied. But the way I see it, we won because we were fighting a bunch of complete idiots!

After all, the British strategy left a lot to be desired. On one side, you had British soldiers standing in plain sight, perfectly lined up, wearing, of all things, bright red coats, while shooting in unison! I'm sure it *looked* quite nice. On the other side, you had our guys, a messy, disorganized hodgepodge of soldiers, hiding behind rocks and trees, shooting back at a bunch of conveniently arranged bright red targets! No wonder we won!

But here's the part I don't get. I can't imagine this was the first time the British fought like that. In other words, despite what I think, the British way of fighting must have actually worked in the past. My only question is—how? For all I know, they'd been doing it that way for hundreds of years and apparently—whether it makes sense to me or not—with a great deal of success. Yet following the same game plan that had worked so well in the past clearly wasn't a good strategy going forward. The British found that out the hard way.

So what about us? We're about to march off, armed with what looks like a great game plan. We have a magic formula that makes sense and has produced phenomenal results in the past. We *expect* to have a lot of success with it in the future. But before we all line up to collect our money, we better stop and think about one obvious problem: How can our strategy keep working after everyone knows about it? If we can't find a good answer, like the British, we may end up as just another easy target.

Well, first, here's some really good news. As it turns out, there are plenty of times when the magic formula doesn't work at all! Isn't that great? In fact, on average, in five months out of each year, the magic formula portfolio does worse than the overall market. But forget months. Often, the magic formula doesn't work for a full year or even more. That's even better!

Imagine buying a book that tells you to invest real money in a group of stocks whose names were spit out by a computer. Imagine diligently watching those stocks each day as they do worse than the market averages over the course of many months or even years. Now imagine deciding enough is enough. No more trusting that stupid book or that mindless computer. You're going to roll up your sleeves and investigate the companies you purchased and the outlook for the businesses you actually own. As we'll find out later, imagine the horror when you realize that if you had only investigated these companies for a few minutes before buying your shares, there is no way you would have touched many of them. Finally, despite awful performance and the disagreeable prospects of the stocks that you own, imagine vowing to continue following the advice of that stupid book and that mindless computer!

But why even worry about all this? After all, the magic formula works. We proved it last chapter! We're going to do really well, so there's no need to worry about months or years of poor performance. And though that sounds right, unfortunately, looking at the statistics for only our very successful 17-year test period, it turns out there's actually plenty to worry about.

The magic formula portfolio fared poorly relative to the market averages in 5 out of every 12 months tested. For full-year periods, the magic formula failed to beat the market averages once every four years.* For one out of every six periods tested, the magic formula did poorly for more than two years in a row. During those wonderful 17 years for the magic formula, there were even some periods when the formula did worse than the overall market for three years in a row!

Think it's easy to stick with a formula that hasn't worked for several years? Do you think the typical reaction goes something like "I know this hasn't worked for a long time," or "I know I just lost a lot of money," but "Let's keep doing what we're doing!"? I assure you, it is not.

---

*Annual returns were calculated from January 1988 to January 1989, February 1988 to February 1989, and so on, through the end of 2004. In all, 193 separate one-year periods were examined.

Take, for example, the case of the author with the best-selling investment book. For his book, the author tested dozens of stock-picking formulas over a period of many decades to determine which of those strategies had beaten the market over the long run. The book was excellent and well-reasoned. The author then opened a *mutual fund* based on buying only those stocks picked by the most successful formula of the dozens he had tested.

The fund then proceeded to perform worse than the major market averages for two of its first three years. For one of those years, the fund underperformed the market average by 25 percent! After three years, the fund was performing poorly relative to competing funds and the best-selling author—the guy who did the tests, the guy who wrote the book—decided to sell his fund management company to somebody else! In fairness, I don't think the author gave up on his formula, but clearly he saw better opportunities elsewhere! Had he known that that same fund, the one managed strictly according to his formula, would come back over the next three years to be one of the top-performing mutual funds since the time of its inception (even including the tough first few years), perhaps he would have stuck with it longer!

But that's not unusual. The unpredictability of Mr. Market's moods and the pressures of competing with other money managers can make it really hard to stick with a strategy that hasn't worked for years. That goes for any strategy, no matter how sensible and regardless of how good the long-term track record is. Let's take a look at the experience of a good friend of mine who happens to be the "smartest money manager I know." Though he doesn't automatically buy stocks that his computer-based formula spits out, he does follow a disciplined strategy of choosing companies to buy only from the list of companies his formula ranks the highest.

He used this strategy very successfully for 10 years at his previous investment firm, and nine years ago he set out to form his own money management firm using the same basic principles. Business wasn't too good for the first three or four years, as the same strategy that had been so successful in the past drastically underperformed the returns of competing money management firms and the major market averages. Nevertheless, the "smartest money manager I know" strongly believed that his strategy still made tremendous sense in the long run and that he should continue following the same course as always. Unfortunately, his clients disagreed. The vast majority of them ran for the exits, pulling their money away in large numbers, most likely to give it to a manager who, unlike my friend, "knew what he was doing."

As you guessed, they should have stuck around. The last five or six years have been so good for my friend and his strategy that now the investment record of his firm since its inception (once again, including those tough first few years) has trounced the returns of the major market averages over the comparable time frame. Today it stands among the top of only a small handful of firms with extraordinary investment records out of the thousands of investment firms on Wall Street. To prove that sometimes good things *do* come to those who wait, my friend's firm now manages over $10 billion for hundreds of clients. Too bad that, in the face of several years of underperformance, most choose not to wait. Only four original clients remain.*

So what's the point? The point is that if the magic formula worked all the time, everyone would probably use it. If everyone used it, it would probably stop working. So many people would be buying the shares of the bargain-priced stocks selected by the magic formula that the prices of those shares would be pushed higher almost immediately. In other words, if everyone used the formula, the bargains would disappear and the magic formula would be ruined!

That's why we're so lucky the magic formula isn't that great. It doesn't work all the time. In fact, it might

---

*Luckily, I'm one of them! (Though, as his friend, I probably *had* to stick around.)

not work for years. Most people just won't wait that long. Their *investment time horizon* is too short. If a strategy works in the long run (meaning it sometimes takes three, four, or even five years to show its stuff), most people won't stick with it. After a year or two of performing worse than the market averages (or earning lower returns than their friends), most people look for a new strategy—usually one that *has* done well over the past few years.

Even professional money managers who *believe* their strategy will work over the long term have a hard time sticking with it. After a few years of poor performance relative to the market or to their competitors, the vast majority of clients and investors just leave! That's why it's hard to stay with a strategy that doesn't follow along with everyone else's. As a professional manager, if you do poorly while everyone else is doing well, you run the risk of losing all your clients and possibly your job!

Many managers feel the only way to avoid that risk is to invest pretty much the way everyone else does. Often this means owning the most popular companies, usually the ones whose prospects look most promising over the next few quarters or the next year or two.

Perhaps now you're beginning to see why most everyone else *won't* be using the magic formula. Though some may take it out for a spin, most won't last past the first few months or years of poor performance. As we discussed back in Chapter 1, you're also beginning to see why all that having to *believe* stuff is so important. If you don't believe that the magic formula will work for you, you'll most likely quit before it has a chance to work! At least, that's where the statistics over the last 17 years seem to point. The magic formula works—long-term annual returns of double, or in some cases almost triple, the returns of the market averages—only those good returns can get pretty lumpy. Over shorter periods, it may work or it may not. When it comes to the magic formula, "shorter" periods can often mean years, not days or months. In a strange but logical way, that's the good news.

Good news, that is, if you believe enough in the magic formula to stick with it over the long term. But to truly stick with a strategy that hasn't worked in years and years, you're going to have to really believe in it deep down in your bones. Sure, the spectacular track record of the magic formula will help, but let's see what your bones think of the next chapter.

## Quick Summary

1. The magic formula appears to work very well over the long term.

2. The magic formula often doesn't work for several years in a row.

3. Most investors won't (or can't) stick with a strategy that hasn't worked for several years in a row.

4. For the magic formula to work for you, you must believe that it will work and maintain a long-term investment horizon.

5. If it wasn't for this chapter, the next chapter would be the most important chapter in the book.

# Chapter Nine

"**V**OMIT UNDER THE 3EM-SPACES AND RUN!"

Now there's a saying you don't hear every day. The main reason you don't hear it much is pretty straightforward. Over time, the phrase has lost all of its meaning. In fact, I really only needed it to pass my eighth-grade course in print shop.

You see, old-time printers used to set type by hand and actually picked letters individually out of a box. To pass the course, my fellow middle schoolers and I were forced to memorize the location of these letters. The letters in the bottom row were V-U-T, then something called a 3em-space, followed by the letters A-R. We remembered the order by the catchy phrase "*Vomit under the 3em-spaces and run!*"

With the advent of computers, my little memory device—and print shop, for that matter—is now useless. Of course, the world has changed a lot since I was in middle school. No one teaches print shop anymore. Thankfully, though, some subjects haven't changed. Math class, for one, is still pretty much the same. As investors, that's really important to know.

That's because, in order for the magic formula to make us money in the long run, the principles behind it must appear not only sensible and logical, but timeless. Otherwise, there is no way we'll be able to "hang on" when our short-term results turn against us. As simple as it may seem, *knowing* that two plus two always equals four can be a pretty powerful concept. No matter how many people tell us differently, no matter how long they tell us, and no matter how smart all those people appear to be, we are unlikely to waver in our conviction. In a similar way, our level of confidence in the magic formula will determine whether we can hang on to a strategy that may be both unpopular and unsuccessful for seemingly long periods of time.

So what is it about the magic formula that makes sense—so much sense, in fact, that we won't waver when things turn against us? Well, let's take another look.

The magic formula chooses companies through a ranking system. Those companies that have both a high return on capital and a high earnings yield are the ones that the formula ranks as best. Put more simply, the formula is systematically helping us find *above-average companies* that we can buy at *below-average prices*.

That certainly sounds logical and sensible. If, indeed, that's what we're really doing, it also sounds like a strategy we can truly believe in. So, let's go step-by-step and see whether that's true.

First, why are companies that earn a high return on capital so special? What kind of companies is our formula telling us to buy? What makes them above average? To understand the answers to those questions, let's go back and check in with our old friend Jason.

Last year, as you may remember, was a pretty good year for Jason's business. Each of his gum shops earned $200,000. Since he only had to invest $400,000 to build each store (including inventory, store displays, etc.), that meant that his return on capital for opening a gum shop was a pretty impressive 50 percent ($200,000 divided by $400,000). So what does that mean?

*Most people and most businesses can't find an investment that will earn a 50 percent annual return.* If the past year is a good guideline and Jason's company can really earn 50 percent a year on its money by simply opening another store, that makes Jason's Gum Shops a pretty special business. Think about that. Having the opportunity to invest your money and earn 50 percent per year is pretty rare. While it's true that there is no guarantee that Jason's new stores (or his old stores) will continue to earn 50 percent returns each year on their original cost, last year's high returns may be a good indicator of the opportunity to earn high returns from investing in that same business going forward.

If that's true and Jason's Gum Shops can continue to earn high returns from its investments in old and new stores, that's really good news for Jason. First, that may mean that the profits from Jason's business don't have to just sit there. While Jason's Gum Shops could take those earnings and invest in a government bond paying 6 percent per year, they have a much better option. The company can take those earnings and invest them in a new store. So not only will the original investment in the first store continue to earn 50 percent per year, but Jason's Gum Shops has the chance to invest the *profits* from the first store in a new store that may also earn 50 percent a year!

*This opportunity to invest profits at high rates of return is very valuable.* For example, if Jason's Gum Shops earned $200,000 last year, Jason has a few options. He can distribute that money to the shareholders of the business (the shareholders can then invest that money however they choose). If the business doesn't change much this coming year, Jason's Gum Shops will earn $200,000 again. That may be a fine outcome.

But if, instead, Jason's Gum Shops takes its $200,000 in profits and invests them in government bonds paying 6 percent (3.6 percent after taxes at a 40 percent rate), Jason's business will earn $207,200 this coming year ($200,000 from the store and $7,200 in after-tax profits from interest on the bond). Though earnings would be higher than last year, the growth rate in earnings would not be very high.

But here's where the big bucks roll in. If Jason takes that same $200,000 in profits and can invest it in a new store that earns a 50 percent annual return,* the earnings for Jason's Gum Shops will grow to $300,000 in the coming year ($200,000 from the original store and an additional $100,000 from the investment in the new store). Going from $200,000 in earnings last year to $300,000 in the coming year would represent a 50 percent earnings growth rate in one year!

In other words, *owning a business that has the opportunity to invest some or all of its profits at a very high rate of return can contribute to a very high rate of earnings growth*!

---

*Assume for this example that we can invest in half a store (though a new store costs $400,000).

So now we know two important things about businesses that can earn a high return on capital. First, businesses that can earn a high return on capital may also have the opportunity to invest their profits at very high rates of return. Since most people and businesses can invest their money at only average rates of return, this opportunity is something special. Second, as we just learned, the ability to earn a high return on capital may also contribute to a high rate of earnings growth. Certainly, that's good news for the companies chosen by the magic formula.

But that still leaves us with one obvious question. If a business like Jason's really can make 50 percent a year by opening a gum shop, why won't other people see that and start opening their own gum shops?

That would mean more competition for Jason's Gum Shops. More competition could mean that Jason will sell less gum in each of *his* stores. More competition could mean that Jason must lower his prices to attract business. More competition could mean that someone builds a better gum shop. In short, more competition could mean lower profits going forward for Jason's Gum Shops.

In fact, that's how our system of *capitalism* works. Good businesses attract competition. Even if competing gum shops open up and the return on capital from opening a new Jason's gum store drops to 40 percent, the threat to future profits might not end there. Earning 40 percent annual returns from opening a gum shop is still quite good. People might see those 40 percent annual returns from opening a gum shop as very attractive and decide to open their own gum shops. Then, due to the increased competition, returns may fall all the way to 30 percent per year from building a new gum shop.

But even there it might not stop! Earning 30 percent a year on an investment is also good. More competition could continue to drive down future returns on capital from new stores and from old stores that are already built. This whole capitalism thing could result in profits continuing to spiral downward until the annual returns on capital from owning gum stores isn't so great anymore. Some system!

But here's the thing. If capitalism is such a tough system, how does the magic formula find us companies that are able to earn a high return on capital in the first place? To earn a high return on capital even for one year, it's likely that, at least temporarily, there's something special about that company's business. Otherwise, competition would already have driven down returns on capital to lower levels.

It could be that the company has a relatively new business concept (perhaps a candy store that sells only gum), or a new product (like a hot video game), or a better product (such as an iPod that's smaller and easier to

use than competitors' products), a good *brand* name
(people will happily pay more for Coke than for Joe's
Cola, so Coke can charge more than Joe's and continue
to earn a high return on capital despite having competition), or a company could have a very strong competitive
position (eBay was one of the first auction web sites and
has more buyers and sellers than anyone else, so it's
hard for new auction sites to offer the same benefits to
customers).

In short, *companies that achieve a high return on capital
are likely to have a special advantage of some kind. That special advantage keeps competitors from destroying the ability to
earn above-average profits.*

Businesses that don't have anything special going for
them (such as new or better products, well-known brand
names, or strong competitive positions) are likely to earn
only average or below-average returns on capital. If there's
nothing special about a company's business, then it's
easy for someone to come in and start a competing business. If a business is earning a high return on capital and
it's easy to compete, eventually someone will! They'll
keep competing until returns on capital are driven down
to average levels.

But the magic formula doesn't choose companies with
average returns on capital. It doesn't choose companies

with below-average returns on capital, either. (Businesses like Just Broccoli are unlikely to earn a high return on capital for even one year!)

So *by eliminating companies that earn ordinary or poor returns on capital, the magic formula starts with a group of companies that have a high return on capital.*

Sure, some of the companies chosen by the magic formula won't be able to maintain their high return on capital. As we just learned, businesses with high returns on capital tend to attract competition. Also, even mediocre businesses can have a good year or two and temporarily achieve a high return on capital.

But, *on average,* the high-return-on-capital companies chosen by the magic formula are more likely to have the opportunity to reinvest a portion of their profits at high rates of return. They are more likely to have the ability to achieve high rates of earnings growth. They are also more likely to have some special competitive advantage that will allow them to continue to earn an above-average return on capital. *In other words, on average, the magic formula is finding us good companies!*

And what does the magic formula do with this group of good companies . . . ?

*It tries to buy them at bargain prices!*

The formula chooses only good companies that also have a high earnings yield. A high earnings yield means that the formula will buy only those companies that earn a lot compared to the price we are paying.

Hmmm . . . buying *above-average companies at below average prices,* it sounds like it should work!

But how do your bones feel about that?

## Quick Summary

1. Most people and businesses can't find investments that will earn very high rates of return. A company that can earn a high return on capital is therefore very special.

2. Companies that earn a high return on capital may also have the opportunity to invest some or all of their profits at a high rate of return. This opportunity is very valuable. It can contribute to a high rate of earnings growth.

3. Companies that achieve a high return on capital are likely to have a special advantage of some kind. That special advantage keeps competitors from destroying the ability to earn above-average profits.

4. By eliminating companies that earn ordinary or poor returns on capital, the magic formula starts

with a group of companies that have a high return on capital. It then tries to buy these above-average companies at below-average prices.

5. Since the magic formula makes overwhelming sense, we should be able to stick with it during good times and bad.

And finally,

6. If you must vomit under the 3em-spaces, don't forget to *run*!

# Chapter Ten

I LOVE SAILING.

I'm not very good at sailing.

I know this, not just from the fact that my wife and kids are scared to go with me, but from hard experience. Once, through a slight miscalculation of wind and water speed, I was 20 feet away from being slammed by a barge at least three football fields long. I remember this quite well, because I had my wife as a passenger (who hates boats anyway) while I was busy pulling the starter cord on my little five-horsepower outboard engine (darn thing never works when you really need it) as the giant barge blasted its horn for me to get out of the way.

Usually sailboats have the right of way over motor-boats, but since 9-billion-pound barges don't steer all that quickly, the right-of-way thing gets switched around (good to keep in mind if it ever comes up). So there I was, repeatedly pulling the worthless starter cord while trying to act like I had everything under control (just so my wife's last words wouldn't be "I hate this stupid boat!"), when a final puff of wind helped us sail out of danger.

I'm recounting this story not because I enjoy sailing alone. I actually like having company (preferably brave or blind company). I'm telling you this because even though I'm clearly not a good sailor, I still love sailing. And that's the same way many people feel about investing in the stock market. They may not be particularly good at it, or they may not know whether they are any good at it, but there's something about the process or the experience that they enjoy.

For some of these people, investing by using a magic formula may take away some of that fun. I understand this. There are also people who are good or would be good at picking individual stocks—without using a magic formula. And that's fine, too. The next chapter should give both groups an idea of what they'll need to know if they want to be successful at picking stocks on their own. It should also show them how the *principles* behind the magic formula can still be used to guide individual invest-ment decisions. But before even thinking about whether to go forward investing with or without the magic formula, there are still a few more things you should know.

First, the magic formula has a better track record than I've been letting on. I didn't reveal this good news earlier for a reason. A good track record is not why you should want to follow the magic formula. A good track record is not why you will have good results in the future. A good track record is not why you will keep following the magic formula even when results turn against you. The truth is that a good track record only helps once you understand *why* the track record is so good. Now that you do—simply put, *the magic formula makes perfect sense*—I can trust you not to get carried away with a little more good news.

As you recall, the magic formula was tested over a recent 17-year period. A portfolio of approximately 30 stocks selected by the magic formula was held throughout that time, with each individual stock selection held for a period of one year. Performance was then measured over 193 separate one-year periods.* The stock portfolios

---

*Performance was measured from January 1988 to January 1989, then February 1988 to February 1989, then March 1988 to March 1989, and so on, for 193 one-year periods ending December 31, 2004. This is commonly referred to as 193 *rolling* one-year periods. Measuring three-year rolling periods would mean measuring performance from January 1988 to January 1991, February 1988 to February 1991, and so on.

chosen by the magic formula usually beat the market averages, but there were one-, two-, and even three-year-long periods when this was not the case. This created the risk that investors might give up on the formula before it had a chance to work its magic.

As we discussed, over one-year periods, the magic formula stock portfolios underperformed the market averages in one out of every four years tested. Following the formula for any two-year period in a row (starting with any month during the 17 years), the magic formula underperformed the market averages in one out of every six periods tested. Remember, while that may not sound all that bad, underperforming for two years in a row is actually pretty hard to take! But here comes the good news. Following the formula for any three-year period in a row, the magic formula beat the market averages *95 percent of the time* (160 out of 169 three-year periods tested)!*

But that's not all! Over three-year periods, if you followed the magic formula, you would *never* have lost money. That's right. Sticking with the magic formula for any three-year period during those 17 years, you would have made money 100 percent of the time (169 out of 169

*There are fewer three-year periods tested than one-year periods because the last three-year period that could be tested started in January 2002 and ended December 31, 2004. The last one-year period started in January 2004.

three-year periods).* Of the 169 separate three-year periods tested, the *worst* return for the magic formula was a *gain of 11 percent*. The *worst* return over a three-year period for the market averages was a *loss of 46 percent*. That's a pretty big difference!

But that's still not all. All those numbers you just read about were based on the results achieved by choosing from only the largest 1,000 stocks (those with a market value over $1 billion). The results from choosing from the largest 3,500 stocks (market values over $50 million), a group of stocks individual investors can generally buy, were even better. *Every* three-year period tested (169 of 169) was positive for the magic formula portfolios, and *every* three-year period *beat* the market averages (169 out of 169). That's right. *The magic formula beat the market averages in* every *single period!* Hey, maybe there *is* something to this magic formula, after all!†

But can we really expect such great results without taking much risk? Well, the answer often depends on how you choose to look at risk.‡ Although over the last 50

---

*In other words, during our 17-year test period, the magic formula portfolios were *still* profitable even when they didn't *beat* the market.

†With this group of 3,500 companies, the *worst* three-year return for the magic formula portfolios was a *gain* of 35 percent. For the market averages, the worst three-year return was a *loss* of 45 percent!

‡Though, in this case, the magic formula looks pretty darn good no matter how we choose to measure risk.

years professors in the financial field have come up with interesting ways to measure or compare the risks of different investment strategies, most of these involve measuring risk in a way that should have no meaning to you. This is true especially if you choose to invest with a truly long-term time horizon. When thinking about risk, rather than making things unnecessarily complicated, there are really two main things you should want to know about an investment strategy:

1. *What is the risk of losing money following that strategy over the long term?*
2. *What is the risk that your chosen strategy will perform worse than alternative strategies over the long term?*

So how does the magic formula stack up under this definition of *risk?* Since it is fairly easy to design an investment strategy to *equal* the return of the market averages* (and yet, as we'll discuss later, most professional investors do even worse than the market averages), we can, at the very least, make a reasonable comparison of these two simple strategies. So let's see.

During our test period and using even a relatively short three-year time frame, the magic formula strategy

*Such as an investment in an *index fund* or an *exchange-traded fund* (*ETF*).

did pretty darn well. The returns from the magic formula strategy were far superior to the returns of the market averages. The magic formula strategy *never* lost money.* The magic formula strategy *beat* the market averages over almost every single three-year period tested. In short, the magic formula strategy achieved *better results with less risk* than the market averages.

Though sticking with the magic formula strategy for even three years paid off incredibly well during our test period, this may not always be the case. Even superior investment strategies may take a long time to show their stuff. If an investment strategy truly makes sense, the longer the time horizon you maintain, the better your chances for ultimate success. Time horizons of 5, 10, or even 20 years are ideal.

Though not easy to do, even maintaining a three- to five-year horizon for your stock market investments should give you a large advantage over most investors. It is also the minimum time frame for any meaningful comparison of the risks and results of alternative investment strategies.

We now have a better understanding of just how powerful and low risk the magic formula truly is, but we still

---

*The market averages lost money in 12 percent of the three-year periods tested. Of course, despite the 100 percent success rate of the magic formula during the test period, *it is almost certain that the magic formula strategy will have negative performance periods in the future.*

have one problem left to solve before we can move on to the next chapter. It has to do with our old friend Mr. Market, and maintaining a proper time horizon plays a key role here, too.

As you may recall from the first day of business school in Chapter 4, it is Mr. Market's constantly changing emotional state that creates the bargain opportunities that the magic formula is able to put to its advantage. But these same emotions create a problem. If Mr. Market is so unstable, how can we be sure that he will eventually pay a fair price for our bargain purchases? If we don't eventually get a fair price from Mr. Market, a bargain could remain a bargain forever (or worse, become even more of a bargain!).

So here's the other thing you *need* to know about Mr. Market:

- Over the short term, Mr. Market acts like a wildly emotional guy who can buy *or sell stocks at depressed or inflated prices.*
- Over the long run, it's a completely different story: *Mr. Market gets it right.*

Yep. Over the long term, crazy Mr. Market is actually a very rational fellow. It may take a few weeks or a few months, and not infrequently a few years, but eventually

Mr. Market will pay a *fair* price for our shares. I actually give a guarantee to my MBA students at the beginning of each semester. I guarantee them that if they do a good job valuing a company, Mr. Market will eventually agree with them. I tell them that, though it can occasionally take longer, if their analysis is correct, two to three years is usually all the time they'll have to wait for Mr. Market to reward their bargain purchases with a fair price.

How can this be? Isn't Mr. Market an emotional basket case? Well, although it's true that Mr. Market can often be ruled by emotion over the short term, over time facts and reality take over. If the price of a stock has been beaten down unfairly in the short term by an overly emotional Mr. Market (this could happen, for instance, when a company announces some bad news or is expected to receive some bad news in the near future), a few things can take place.

First, there are a lot of smart people out there. If the price offered by Mr. Market is truly a bargain, some of these smart people will eventually recognize the bargain opportunity, buy stock, and push the price closer to fair value. This doesn't have to happen right away. Sometimes uncertainty about the prospects for a particular company over the near term will keep potential buyers away. Sometimes the influence of emotions can last for years. But here's the thing. Eventually, the problem or the reason for the emotional reaction is resolved. It could be a positive resolution or a negative one. It doesn't really matter. If there is uncertainty about a company's earnings over the next two or three years, by waiting long enough we eventually find out the answer (even if this takes the full two or three years!). Once the reality of the situation is known, smart investors will buy stock if the bargain opportunity still exists.

Second, even if these so-called "smart" people don't recognize the bargain opportunity and buy shares, there are other ways that stock prices can move toward fair value. Often companies buy back their own shares. If a company believes its shares are undervalued, the management of the company can decide that it is a good investment to use its own cash and repurchase some of the company's shares.* So this action of companies buying back their own shares is another activity that causes prices to rise and may help eliminate some bargain opportunities.

If that doesn't work, there are still other ways that share prices tend to move toward fair value. Remember, a share of stock represents an ownership interest in an actual company. Anyone who buys all of the shares

---

*This would reduce the amount of cash the company had, but it would also reduce the number of shares outstanding of the company. If ownership of the company is distributed among fewer shares, each remaining shareholder would own a larger percentage interest in the company.

outstanding would then own the entire company. Often, if a bargain opportunity persists for too long, another company or a large investment firm may decide to make a bid for all of the shares outstanding and purchase the entire company. Sometimes even the possibility that a buyer for the whole company may emerge can cause share prices to rise toward fair value.

In short, over time the interaction of all of these things—smart investors searching for bargain opportunities, companies buying back their own shares, and the takeover or possibility of a takeover of an entire company—work together to move share prices toward fair value. Sometimes this process works quickly, and sometimes it can take several years.

*Although over the short term, Mr. Market may set stock prices based on emotion, over the long term, it is the value of the company that becomes most important to Mr. Market.*

*This means that if you buy shares at what you believe to be a bargain price and you are right, Mr. Market will eventually agree and offer to buy those shares at a fair price. In other words, bargain purchases will be rewarded. Though the process doesn't always work quickly, two to three years is usually enough time for Mr. Market to get things right.*

So now that we have all that good news out of the way, let's see if we can sail through the next chapter without hitting anything.

## Quick Summary

1. The magic formula works. It works even better than I let on before.
2. The magic formula achieved its far superior results with far less risk than the market averages.
3. Although over the short term Mr. Market may price stocks based on emotion, over the long term Mr. Market prices stocks based on their *value*.
4. If you couldn't vomit under the 3em-spaces, try sailing with me.

# Chapter Eleven

So THE MAGIC FORMULA ISN'T YOUR THING. The high returns, the low risk, the simplicity, the logic—these things mean nothing to you. You want—in fact, you *need*—to pick stocks all by yourself! No one, and especially no silly formula, is going to stand in your way. You're out there on the ledge, and there's no use talking you down! Don't worry. I get it, and that's just fine. But to borrow from something I once wrote, remember this:

*Choosing individual stocks without any idea of what you're looking for is like running through a dynamite factory with a burning match. You may live, but you're still an idiot.*

So how *can* you pick stocks intelligently? What *should* you be looking for? Even if you've decided not to follow the magic formula, how can you *still* use it to keep from blowing yourself up? Well, glad you asked. Let's see.

As we already know, the magic formula picks stocks that have both a high earnings yield and a high return on capital. For earnings yield, the formula looks for companies that earn a lot compared to the price *we* have to pay. For return on capital, the formula looks for companies that earn a lot compared to how much *the company* has to pay to buy the assets that created those earnings. To calculate these ratios, the magic formula doesn't look at future earnings. That's too hard. The magic formula uses *last year's* earnings.

The funny thing is, that seems like the wrong thing to do. The value of a company comes from how much money it will earn for us in the future, not from what happened in the past. If a company earned $2 per share last year, but will earn only $1 per share this year and even less in the future, using last year's earnings to calculate earnings yield and return on capital will be very misleading. But that's precisely what the magic formula does!

In fact, often the near-term prospects for the companies selected by the magic formula don't look so good. In many cases, the outlook for the next year or two is downright ugly. But that's one reason the magic formula can find companies whose prices *seem* like bargains. The magic formula uses *last* year's earnings. If, instead, estimates for this year's or next year's earnings were used, many of the companies selected by the magic formula might not look like such bargains at all!

So what *should* we be doing? Ideally, better than blindly plugging in *last year's* earnings to the formula, we should be plugging in estimates for earnings in a *normal* year.* Of course, last year's earnings could be representative of a normal year, but last year may not have been typical for a number of reasons. Earnings could have been higher than normal due to extraordinarily favorable conditions that may not be repeated in most years. Alternatively, there may have been a temporary problem with the company's operations, and earnings may have been lower than in a normal year.

Plugging in estimates for *next year's* earnings to our formula may suffer from the same problem. Next year may not be typical. So one solution might be to look ahead even further to our estimates of what earnings will be three or four years from now in a normal or average environment. Short-term issues that may have affected last year's earnings or that may affect earnings over the next year or two could then largely be eliminated from our thinking.

---

*A normal year is one in which nothing extraordinary or unusual is happening within the company, its industry, or the overall economy.

In this ideal world, we would then be able to take our estimates of normal earnings and calculate earnings yield and return on capital. Using the principles of the magic formula, we could look for companies that had both a high earnings yield and a high return on capital based on normal earnings. Of course, we would also need to assess how confident we were in our estimates and make a judgment on whether those earnings were likely to grow in the future.* We could then compare the earnings yield based on normal earnings to a risk-free 6 percent government bond and to our other investment opportunities.

Does that sound hard to do? Well, it is. Yet it's not impossible. There *are* people who can do this type of analysis. In fact, this is precisely the way my partners and I use the principles behind the magic formula to make our own investment decisions. But *if you can't* do this type of analysis (and here comes the main point of this chapter):

> *You have no business investing in*
> *individual stocks on your own!*

That's right. Forget about it!

But wait a second. The magic formula does pretty well, and it just uses last year's earnings. It doesn't make

---

*As well as whether there was an honest management team that would reinvest those profits wisely.

any estimates, and it doesn't even do any thinking. How come the magic formula gets to pick stocks and I'm telling most of you to just forget about picking individual stocks on your own?

Well, the answer is that the magic formula doesn't pick individual stocks, either. It picks many stocks at one time. Looking at a whole portfolio of stocks, it turns out that using last year's earnings is often a good indicator of what earnings will look like in the future. Of course, for individual companies, this may not be the case. But on average, last year's earnings will often provide a pretty good estimate for normal earnings going forward.

That's why, if we actually use the magic formula, we'll want to own 20 or 30 stocks at one time. In the magic formula's case, we *want* the average (that is, the average return for a portfolio of stocks chosen by the magic formula). Since average results for the magic formula will, hopefully, mean extraordinary investment returns, owning many different stocks chosen by the magic formula should help ensure that we stay pretty close to that average.

By now, I hope I've convinced 99 percent of you to just stick with the magic formula. But for those few who still hope to develop a winning strategy for picking individual stocks, there is something that you should consider. Even professional research analysts and money managers have a tough time making accurate earnings predictions for individual companies. For these professionals, making accurate predictions for 20 or 30 companies at the same time is even harder. It won't be any easier for you.

So here's my suggestion. If you still want to buy individual stocks despite all the warnings, don't even try to make a lot of predictions. Limit your stock investments to a small number of "good" companies that are available at bargain levels. For those few investors who *are* capable of estimating normal earnings several years into the future and placing values on businesses, owning just a handful of bargain-priced stocks is the best way to go. As a general rule of thumb, if you are truly doing good research and have a good understanding of the companies that you purchase, owning just five to eight stocks in different industries can safely make up at least 80 percent of your total portfolio.*

But what if you aren't an expert at valuing businesses and making predictions? Isn't there still some way you can intelligently play the stock-picking game? While it may not be smart to hang out in dynamite factories, so what? Some people would rather have a blast. Well, okay. There is a compromise strategy, and it makes sense, too. But you're still going to need the magic formula—there's just no way around that (not in this book, anyway).

*Not sure that makes sense? See the box at the end of the chapter!

Here it is. Rather than just blindly choosing stocks that catch your fancy or blindly accepting the output of the magic formula, how about combining both strategies? Start with the magic formula and put together a list of top-ranked stocks. Then choose a few of your favorites by whatever method you want. You must, however, choose solely from the top 50 or 100 stocks as ranked by the magic formula.* Using this method, you should still place at least 10 to 30 stocks in your portfolio (the lower end of this range if you actually know something about evaluating businesses and the higher end if you are choosing stocks based on birth signs). And that should do it.

Now for the summary:

1. *Most people have no business investing in individual stocks on their own!*
2. Reread summary point number 1.
3. But if you must . . . and you *can* actually predict normalized earnings several years down the road, use those estimates to figure out earnings yield and return on capital. Then, use the principles of the magic formula to look for good companies at bargain prices based on your estimates of normal earnings.

---

*Don't worry, we'll learn how to easily compile a list of top-ranked stocks later.

4. If you truly understand the business that you own *and* have a high degree of confidence in your normalized earnings estimates, owning five to eight bargain-priced stocks in different industries can be a safe and effective investment strategy.

5. *Most people have no business investing in individual stocks on their own!* (Did I already mention that?)

---

How can owning just five to eight stocks possibly be a safe strategy? Think of it this way.* You're a successful local businessman who has just sold off his business for $1 million. You want to invest that money wisely so that you can safely earn a good return over time. You have the opportunity to reinvest the proceeds from the sale of your business by buying an ownership stake in some of the other businesses in town. You have some understanding of about 30 of those businesses, and your plan is to invest in companies that you understand well, that have a good future, and that are available at a reasonable price.

For those companies about which you feel most confident in your ability to make predictions, you project what normal earnings should be several years

*To borrow an analogy from one of the world's greatest investors.

down the road. You also look for companies that you believe will be able to continue in business for many years and for companies that should have the ability to grow their earnings over time. Then you calculate earnings yield and return on capital based on your estimates for each of those companies. Of course, your goal is to find good businesses that can be purchased at bargain prices. On the basis of your analysis, you select your five favorites and invest $200,000 in each.

Does that sound like risky behavior? It would be if you had no idea how to read financial statements or evaluate individual businesses. But if you do have that ability, is buying a stake in your five favorite businesses enough? Would owning a stake in your eight favorites be better? I think most people, especially those who view stocks as long-term ownership stakes in actual businesses, would think that spreading that $1 million among investment stakes in five to eight bargain-priced businesses in varying industries would qualify as prudent behavior.

At least, that's the view I take with *my* investment portfolio. The more confidence I have in each one of my stock picks, the fewer companies I need to own in my portfolio to feel comfortable. Most investors view stocks and the construction of stock portfolios differently, however.

Somehow, when ownership interests are divided into shares that bounce around with Mr. Market's moods, individuals and professionals start to think about and measure risk in strange ways. When short-term thinking and overly complicated statistics get involved, owning many companies that you know very little about starts to sound safer than owning stakes in five to eight companies that have good businesses, predictable futures, and bargain prices. In short, for the few who have the ability, knowledge, and time to predict normal earnings and evaluate individual stocks, owning less can actually be more—more profits, more safety . . . and more fun!

# Chapter Twelve

THERE'S SOMETHING ABOUT THE TOOTH FAIRY. For some reason, I've never been able to fully fess up to my kids about what's really going on there. Perhaps I just want them to hold on to their childhood for as long as possible, or maybe I just want to cherish the innocence of that stage of their lives. But whatever it is, I've been a rock while under the most intense of interrogations concerning my whereabouts after money has mysteriously appeared under the various pillows in question.

I've had a few close calls, though. I thought the jig was up one day when one of my kids marched home from first grade with some new information (it's scary the kind of things they pick up hanging out in the school yard). It seems a friend, with absolutely no regard for all my years of stonewalling, had spilled the beans. As I was doing all I could to choke back my disappointment, my miniature Sherlock Holmes declared, "I know who the tooth fairy is!" My mind raced for some way out as he continued, "It's Billy Gordon's mother!"

After explaining what a ridiculous logistical and financial nightmare it would be for Billy Gordon's mother to roam the entire world each night collecting teeth and shelling out money, I was able to quell that particular piece of misinformation. And luckily, either because of a lack of investigative instincts or merely because they have learned to humor me over the years, that's the closest any under-age member of my house has come to cracking the case.

But here's a secret I have no problem divulging. In my house, whatever story my kids choose to believe is just fine with me. But in the stock market, there's only one version of the story I want them to know. It's harsh and it's unfair, but we all have to grow up sometime. And it's about time you know it, too. So here it is. When it comes to Wall Street,

*There ain't no tooth fairy!**

---

*Of course, since technically that's a double negative, I still haven't admitted anything!

That's right. On Wall Street, money won't magically appear under your pillow. There's no one to tuck you in, no one to take care of you, and no one you can turn to for good advice. Once you've left the warmth and comfort of your own home, the plain fact is, *you're on your own.*

To see why this is necessarily so, we're going to take our own little walk down Wall Street. But before we set out, let's make a few assumptions. First, you have some money that you would like to invest over the long term. (*Long term,* in this case, means that you will not need this money to cover your normal expenses for at least the next three to five years—and, hopefully, longer.)* Second, you would like to earn as much as possible from your investments, but you are unwilling to take unreasonable risks. Finally, you've heard (and this is generally true) that the stock market offers the best possibility for high investment returns over time, and this is where you would like to put most of your money. So, fine, where do we start?

Well, one typical stop is our friendly neighborhood *stockbroker.* This is an investment professional whose job is to hold your hand and help you invest your money. Your

---

*Since Mr. Market can do anything in the short term, money that you require over the next few years for necessities is best left in the bank. Otherwise, you may be forced to sell to Mr. Market at just the wrong time (for instance, when you need money to cover expenses and a depressed Mr. Market is offering low prices for your shares).

stockbroker will help you choose between individual stocks, bonds, investment funds, and various other investment alternatives. If you have enough money, he or she will even speak with you on the phone, try to understand your needs, and give you suggestions and advice.

But here's the thing. If your stockbroker is like the vast majority, he or she has no idea how to help you! Most get paid a fee to *sell* you a stock or a bond or some other investment product. They don't get paid to make you money. Of course, while it's in their interest for you to be successful and many may be fine, well-intentioned professionals, a stockbroker's main incentive is still to *sell* you something. They are trained to follow rules, understand certain financial terms, and explain various investment products. As for how to make you money in the stock market or anywhere else, forget it!

You might as well just put your money in a *mutual fund*. Now here's the perfect solution for a small investor. A mutual fund is an investment fund that is managed by a professional money manager. The manager usually selects a diverse group of stocks or bonds, generally from 30 to 200 different securities in the same fund. This is a particularly efficient way for a small investor to spread his or her investment capital over a wide group of different investments.

But here, too, there are some problems. As we've discussed before, it's tough to have special insight into many different companies and investment securities. Consequently, owning dozens or even hundreds of positions does not often lead to above-average returns. Then, of course, there is the small matter of fees. Mutual fund management companies need to charge a fee for their services. Basic math says that average returns minus fees equals below-average returns. Not surprisingly, after subtracting fees and other expenses, the vast majority of mutual funds do not beat the market averages over time.

But that's okay. We can just look for mutual funds that have above-average managers. It should be relatively easy to tell whether a manager is above average simply by looking at the fund's track record. The only problem with this strategy is that on average there is *no* relationship between a fund's good past investment record and its future returns. Even companies whose business is to rate mutual funds have a poor record of determining which funds will perform well in the future.

While there are many reasons for this, all of them are difficult to resolve. Mutual fund management companies get paid based on how much money is invested in each fund. A fund with a successful track record will usually attract more money over time. It is usually in the fund's economic interest to accept this money. Once a fund grows larger, it may be hard for the manager to continue with the same strategy that led to the successful returns.

A few good ideas may now be spread even thinner over a larger pile of money. If investment in smaller companies is partially responsible for some of the success, this may no longer be possible in a larger fund. Also, even talented managers have bad stretches of investment performance (just like the magic formula). Conversely, bad managers can have good stretches. Telling which is which, even over periods of several years, is quite difficult. I could go on, but the facts are the facts. A good past investment record isn't much help when predicting future returns, and picking a good manager is likely no easier than picking attractive individual stocks. Then again, if you could pick attractive stocks, you probably wouldn't need the good manager!

So, instead, you might consider investing in a *hedge fund*. These are exclusive private investment funds usually reserved for very wealthy investors. Unfortunately, in most cases, unless you already have at least $500,000 or so to invest, you probably won't even have this option. By law, most hedge funds can only accept investors who can afford to lose large amounts of money. But even if you qualify for this dubious honor, it's not clear that this is a smart way to go.

Hedge funds are investment funds that have more flexibility than most mutual funds. Managers can use the fund's capital and borrowed money to buy a large variety of securities. Generally, they are able to place bets on whether stocks, other securities, or entire market averages will move up or down. Most mutual funds are restricted to making money only when the securities they own go up. A hedge fund's ability to bet up or down over many different securities, often with the aid of borrowed money, is seen as a big advantage over most standard mutual funds. It may be. But most hedge funds charge huge fees—at least 1 percent of assets under management *plus* a 20 percent share of the profits. No doubt attracted by the large fees, thousands of new hedge funds have been created over the past few years. Most will have no chance of justifying their fees. There just aren't that many great managers, and your chances of finding one are quite slim.

So that's why many people just choose to invest in an *index fund.** An index fund is a mutual fund that just tries to *equal* the overall market's return, less a very small fee. These funds pick a market index (perhaps the S&P 500 index of 500 large stocks or the Russell 2000 index, an index that consists of 2,000 somewhat smaller stocks) and buy all of the stocks in that particular index. Although

*Or an exchange-traded fund (ETF), an index fund that trades similar to the way a stock trades.

this strategy won't help you *beat* the market, it will help you achieve returns that are at least close to the market averages.* Since, after taking into account fees and other costs, most other investment choices leave you with much lower returns than index funds, many people who have carefully studied the issue have concluded that settling for average returns is actually a pretty good alternative. In fact, over the last 80 years, average returns from the stock market have meant returns of over 10 percent per year. Not too bad at all.

But what if you want to do better than average? The simple truth is there's no stop on *our* little walk that has an answer for that one. That's because it's pretty much like I told you before: On Wall Street, there is no tooth fairy. Once you leave home, you can put your money under *a professional's* pillow, but chances are, when you wake up, all you'll be left with is lousy performance.

Of course, I know what you're going to ask. Isn't there somewhere you can go? Something you can do? Someone you can turn to?

---

*Also, if you are not investing using a tax-free retirement account and taxes are a concern for you, this strategy will minimize the amount of taxes you must pay because index funds typically do not sell their stock holdings unless a particular security is dropped from the index. This is usually less than 10 percent of the securities in the index in any one year.

Well, it should come as no surprise that after 25 years in the investment business, I've been asked these same questions many times. From time to time, I have been able to recommend a particularly good mutual fund manager or an exceptional hedge fund manager. In all cases, the funds in question have subsequently grown to many times their original size and the investment opportunity has largely vanished in a rather short period of time. I have also tried to help people by giving out an occasional stock tip. However, an occasional stock tip from me is not a very reliable or universally available long-term investment strategy.

So I'm usually at a loss. If you want to do as little as possible and you don't mind doing average, an index fund could be a fine choice. But if you are capable of analyzing businesses and willing to do a fair amount of work, selectively picking individual stocks can be a viable alternative. The only problem is that most people don't have the time or ability to analyze individual companies. As we discussed last chapter, if you don't know how to evaluate businesses and project normal earnings several years into the future, you have no business investing in individual stocks in the first place.

So here's the thing. As unbelievable as it may seem, if you truly want to beat the market, there really is only one good alternative left. After all we've been through, I probably don't have to spell it out for you. But let's just say it rhymes with . . . *bagic mormula.*

That's right. Just like I promised earlier, by following the simple steps outlined at the end of this book, you can use the magic formula to beat the market. You can achieve extraordinary long-term investment returns, and you can achieve those returns with low risk. By following step-by-step, you'll know exactly where to go and what to do. It won't even take much work—just minutes every few months.

But that's not the hard part. The hard part is making sure that you understand *why* the magic formula makes sense. The hard part is continuing to *believe* that the magic formula *still* makes sense even when friends, experts, the news media, and Mr. Market indicate otherwise. Lastly, the hard part is just getting started, though I've tried to make that task as easy as possible.

So, good luck. I truly believe that if you follow the lessons in this book, you will have a great deal of investment success. That's what makes the next chapter so important. After all, if my calculations are correct, you're still going to be left with a pretty big problem. I'm very serious. I mean, what *are* you going to do with all that money?

## Quick Summary

1. On Wall Street, *there ain't no tooth fairy!*
2. Nothing much rhymes with *magic formula*.
3. Your step-by-step instructions for beating the market using the magic formula are coming right after the next chapter.

# Chapter Thirteen

**W**HAT WOULD YOU DO IF YOU HAD A LOT OF MONEY? Of course, I mean what would you do after taking care of your family and those close to you, after providing for retirement and the future of your loved ones, and after putting some aside to buy a few luxuries along the way? What would you do?

Actually, you may well have to answer that question someday. But don't worry. I'm not going to bore you with a pile of statistics. I'm not going to tell you about all the money you could make by using the magic formula. I'm not even going to discuss the whole idea of *compound interest*. That's the one where you invest a relatively small amount of money, earn a reasonable rate of return over time, continually reinvest all the earnings from those investments, and end up with a large amount of money. I'm not going to talk about that.

It's really too bad, though. With the new rules for contributing larger amounts of money to tax-advantaged retirement accounts, it *would* have been a good thing to discuss. As it turns out, starting now and making the maximum allowable contribution to an *IRA*\* for just the next few years, you could turn a relatively small amount of money into a much larger amount. Obviously, with the type of returns achieved by the magic formula in the past, this really could have meant a lot of money for you. But, unfortunately, we're not going to discuss it.

It's truly a shame. By contributing just $28,000 in total over the next six years (the maximum of $4,000 per year in both 2006 and 2007 and then $5,000 per year starting in 2008 for four years†), your retirement account could have grown to over $325,000 at the end of 20 years and over $1.3 million after 30 years. That's if you could achieve an annual return on your investments of 15 percent. Of course, the past record of the magic formula is somewhat better than 15 percent per year, but it would be irresponsible to project some higher annual return far into

---

\*Either a traditional investment retirement account or a Roth IRA.
†Thereafter making no further contributions of any kind.

the future. That's because picking a number like 20 percent per year would turn that initial $28,000* into $752,000 after 20 years and more than $4.3 million after 30 years. At an astronomical rate like 25 percent per year (a return that is still lower than the past returns of one of our portfolios of smaller magic formula stocks), that $28,000 would have become more than $1.6 million in 20 years and over $13.4 million in 30 years.† But who's really counting, and with numbers like that, thank heaven I had the good sense not to mention it.

But I will say this. If you are still in middle school or even high school and you are approached by anyone—and I mean *anyone,* no matter how fancy their scooter or how persuasive their sales pitch—and they want you to purchase a single stick of gum for 25 cents, I have just three words of advice:

---

*From investing the maximum allowable $4,000 per year in an IRA over the next two years and then the increased maximum of $5,000 per year for the following four years equaling $28,000 over the six years.

†It's fascinating to note that if you had decided to contribute $5,000 per year for the remaining 24 years of this 30-year period, rather than stopping contributions after just six years as we did in this example, your IRA account would have grown to approximately $16.5 million after 30 years versus the $13.4 million from just those six contributions. Had we decided to talk about compound interest, the relatively smaller benefit from those last 24 contributions would have illustrated how truly important starting as early as possible is to achieving the full benefits of compounding.

### Don't do it!

I say that not because at any moment you could be forced to stand in the corner with a wad of gum stuck to your nose. I say that because if you understood how a well-invested quarter could possibly turn into more than $200 by the time you hit middle age,* you might not squander so much money on a single stick of gum! You might not spend money on a lot of things. Instead, you might start thinking about *saving money* whenever possible and *spending time* figuring out a good way to invest it. That's what I'm saying.

Unfortunately, one thing I'm not saying is that using the magic formula for your investments going forward will guarantee results similar to the stellar performance of the past. I can't know that.[†] But I can say this:

*I believe that using the magic formula and the principles behind the magic formula to guide your future investments will*

---

*Twenty-five cents invested at a return of 25 percent a year for 30 years would get you more than $200. Of course, I'm not saying you would actually achieve this type of return (as you know, I would never say that).

[†]Though, since the market averages returned roughly 12 percent per year (including dividends) during the course of our 17-year study and my best guess for the market averages going forward is closer to 6 to 10 percent per year, you may want to start by adjusting down your hopes and/or expectations for the future absolute results of using the magic formula by 3 or 4 percent per year as compared to the results found in the study. But, once again, I can't really know.

*remain one of your very best investment alternatives. I believe that if you are able to stick with the magic formula strategy through good periods and bad, you will handily beat the market averages over time. In short, I believe that, even after everyone knows the magic formula, your results will continue to be not only "quite satisfactory," but with a little luck, extraordinary.*

So, here's the deal. If you do end up using the magic formula and if it helps you earn enough money that you feel grateful for your good fortune, you might consider this. In reality, all the time and effort put into stock market investing isn't a very productive use of time. Usually, when you buy or sell shares in a publicly traded company,* you are merely buying from or selling to another shareholder. In other words, the underlying company is not involved. It receives nothing from the transaction.

Many people argue that all this buying and selling activity is, nevertheless, quite useful. Through the buying and selling of shares, these people would argue, an active marketplace for the company's shares is established. Theoretically, if a company needs additional money, it can decide to sell additional shares into this marketplace. It can use the proceeds to pay bills, build factories, or expand in some other way. This is all true. Also, if Jason

---

*A company that files its financial information with the government and whose shares the general public may buy and sell.

decides to expand his gum store chain from 10 stores to 300, he can sell some shares in his new and growing business directly to the public and raise money for the expansion. Since the buyers of Jason's Gum Shop shares know that there will be a marketplace for selling those shares after their initial purchase, Jason may have an easier time raising money for his business. The people who see great value in stock trading are right about this, too.

I'm just not one of those people. Yes, it is nice to have a marketplace. In fact, it's very important. It's just that more than 95 percent of the trading back and forth each day is probably unnecessary. The market would still be fine without almost all of it. The market would certainly be fine without *your* contribution.

In fact, the first day of class each semester, I tell all of my MBA students that I'm about to teach them skills that have limited value. It's not that they won't have the potential to make a lot of money from what they learn. It's that there are probably higher and better uses for their time and intellect. As a consequence, in exchange for teaching them, I always ask my students to find some way to give back.*

So, for you, too, I hope this book and the step-by-step instructions that follow will help you reach all of your

*For some more thoughts, see the box at the end of the chapter.

investment goals. I strongly believe that it will. I also hope that those investment goals will include using some of your good fortune to make a difference in those areas that are important and have meaning to you.

*Good luck.*

There are, of course, many worthwhile things to do with your money in addition to caring for those near and dear to you. Whether it involves supporting medical research, aiding the poor, promoting social justice, or supporting pretty much any worthy cause that you believe in, all would obviously be wonderful choices for your charitable dollars. But since this entire book is about investing your money in places where it can earn a high return on capital, I have one additional thought that you might consider.

It is our education system that nurtures the entrepreneurs, scientists, engineers, technologists, and high-level workforce that help our economy grow and thrive. Over time, the performance of the stock market reflects this progress. Yet it is very clear that we are wasting much of our future potential. In almost every major city in the United States, barely half of entering public school ninth-graders end up graduating from high school. Think about that for a moment. Undoubtedly, there are many reasons for this devastating waste, but the problems, whatever they might be, clearly cut across all grade levels. Many students enter the ninth grade already four and five grade levels behind.

So how *should* we solve this problem? Obviously, teaching young people should be a top priority, and spending money to teach children the skills necessary to become productive members of society should be a great investment. Talk about a high return on capital! Just as obvious is that there are negative costs to doing a bad job—crime, drugs, and welfare, to name a few. So, how *are* we trying to solve this problem?

Under capitalism, it would be pretty straightforward. If we were trying to fix a business like Just Broccoli, we would first try to change a few things. Maybe we would fire bad managers, hire better salespeople, or do some advertising, but eventually, if results didn't improve, we would just close the stores. Under our system of capitalism, companies that can't earn an adequate return on capital eventually go out of business. That's very healthy. Instead of continually throwing money into investments that achieve poor returns, under capitalism money is systematically redirected into businesses that can make productive use of new capital. That's how our economy continues to grow and thrive over time.

So how would you fix the public school system? First, you would try to make some changes. You might fire bad teachers, pay more for good teachers, remove bad principals, and at the end of the day, close bad schools. The money spent on the bad schools would be redirected to schools (public or private) that could get a higher return on the capital spent. Unfortunately, in the case of inner-city public schools, the same problems have been going on for over 40 years and the "fixes" have been going on for just as long!

The difference is this. In capitalism, if the fixes don't work, the business closes. With public schools, this rarely happens. It's almost impossible to fire bad teachers, pay more for good teachers, or close bad schools. In short, there are no penalties for poor performance, incentives for good performance, or consequences for running a poor business.

As a result, money spent on bad teachers or bad schools is almost never redirected to teachers or schools that can achieve higher returns on that capital! So if we want to apply what we have learned about capitalism, any solutions, whether they involve public school reform, charter schools, or voucher programs, need to address these issues. Otherwise, we'll be stuck with a Just Broccoli school system for a long time to come!*

*If you have further interest, some web sites you might consider: successforall.net, alliance forschoolchoice.com, schoolachievement.org, democratsforeducationreform.org.

# Step-by-Step Instructions

Here's the big picture. As you know, the magic formula has achieved excellent results in the past. So our goal is to create an easy-to-follow plan that will help reproduce those good results. But before we adopt any strategy, we need to consider a few things.

First, since the returns reported in this book were based on holding a portfolio of roughly 30 stocks selected by the magic formula, we should make sure that our plan includes holding at least 20 to 30 stocks at one time. Remember, the magic formula works *on average,* so holding many stocks that are ranked highly by the magic formula should help keep us close to that average over time.*

Second, in our tests, each stock was held for a period

---

*Obviously, if you are already good at analyzing businesses and doing your own research and are merely using the magic formula as a guideline to find attractive individual stocks, these diversification rules *do not* apply to you. On the other hand, if you are doing a limited amount of work on individual stocks or no work at all (like most investors), diversifying with 20 or 30 magic formula stocks is *most definitely* the right plan for you.

of one year. Holding stocks for one year is still fine for tax-free accounts. For taxable accounts, we will want to adjust that slightly. For individual stocks in which we are showing a loss from our initial purchase price, we will want to sell a few days *before* our one-year holding period is up. For those stocks with a gain, we will want to sell a day or two *after* the one-year period is up. In that way, all of our gains will receive the advantages of the lower tax rate afforded to long-term capital gains (a maximum 15 percent tax rate under federal guidelines for stocks held more than one year), and all of our losses will receive short-term tax treatment (a deduction against other sources of income that otherwise could have been taxable at rates up to 35 percent). Over time, this minor adjustment can add significantly to our after-tax investment returns.

Lastly, be aware that getting started will be the hardest part. We probably don't want to buy all 30 stocks at once. To reproduce the results from our tests, we will have to work into our magic formula portfolio over the course of our first year of investing. That means adding 5 to 7 stocks to our portfolio every few months until we reach 20 or 30 stocks in our portfolio. Thereafter, as stocks in our portfolio reach the one-year holding mark, we will replace only the 5 to 7 stocks that have been held for one year. If that's a little confusing, don't worry, step-by-step instructions are about to follow.

Now that we have that settled, we need to discuss a

few simple ways to find our magic formula stocks. There are many choices for screening packages to help us sort through the universe of available stocks, both Web-based programs and software programs that utilize the Web for updates. Some of these options are available for free, while others can cost up to $99 per month or even more. Each has advantages and disadvantages based on ease of operation and the reliability, flexibility, and breadth of data sources. Most will generate a reasonable set of magic formula stocks if certain conditions are applied, which are discussed below.

One screening option was created specifically for this book, magicformulainvesting.com. The magicformula investing.com site is designed to emulate the returns achieved in our study as closely as possible. This site is currently available for free. Step-by-step instructions for selecting stocks using magicformulainvest ing.com follow.

Other options include, but are not limited to, the screening packages available at businessweek.com, aaii .com, moneycentral.msn.com, powerinvestor.com, and smartmoney.com. Though these sources are generally fine, and are available either for free or at a reasonable price, they are not specifically designed to generate magic formula stocks. They will only give a rough approximation of the magic formula results because of differences both in the criteria the user can select and the underlying data sources. General screening instructions are available on each site.

## Option 1: MagicFormulaInvesting.com

### Step 1

Go to magicformulainvesting.com.

### Step 2

Follow the instructions for choosing company size (e.g., companies with market capitalizations over $50 million, or over $200 million, or over $1 billion, etc.). For most individuals, companies with market capitalizations above $50 million or $100 million should be of sufficient size.

### Step 3

Follow the instructions to obtain a list of top-ranked magic formula companies.

### Step 4

Buy five to seven top-ranked companies. To start, invest only 20 to 33 percent of the money you intend to invest during the first year (for smaller amounts of capital, lower-priced Web brokers such as foliofn.com, buyandhold.com, and scottrade.com may be a good place to start).

### Step 5

Repeat Step 4 every two to three months until you have invested all of the money you have chosen to allocate to your magic formula portfolio. After 9 or 10 months, this should result in a portfolio of 20 to 30 stocks (e.g., seven stocks every three months, five or six stocks every two months).

## Step 6
Sell each stock after holding it for one year. For taxable accounts, sell winners after holding them a few days more than one year and sell losers after holding them a few days less than one year (as previously described). Use the proceeds from any sale and any additional investment money to replace the sold companies with an equal number of new magic formula selections (Step 4).

## Step 7
Continue this process for many years. *Remember, you must be committed to continuing this process for a minimum of three to five years, regardless of results. Otherwise, you will most likely quit before the magic formula has a chance to work!*

## Step 8
Feel free to write and thank me.

## Option 2: General Screening Instructions

If using any screening option other than magicformula investing.com, you should take the following steps to best approximate the results of the magic formula:

- Use Return on Assets (ROA) as a screening criterion. Set the minimum ROA at 25%. (This will take the place of *return on capital* from the magic formula study.)
- From the resulting group of high ROA stocks, screen for those stocks with the *lowest* Price/Earning (P/E) ratios. (This will take the place of *earnings yield* from the magic formula study.)
- Eliminate all utilities and financial stocks (i.e., mutual funds, banks and insurance companies) from the list.
- Eliminate all foreign companies from the list. In most cases, these will have the suffix "ADR" (for "American Depository Receipt") after the name of the stock.
- If a stock has a very low P/E ratio, say 5 or less, that may indicate that the previous year or the data being used are unusual in some way. You may want to eliminate these stocks from your list. You may also want to eliminate any company that has announced earnings in the last week. (This should help minimize the incidence of incorrect or untimely data.)
- After obtaining your list, follow steps 4 and 8 from the magicformulainvesting.com instruction page.

# Appendix

**IMPORTANT NOTICE:** This appendix is not required reading. To utilize the magic formula strategy successfully, you must understand only two basic concepts. *First, buying good companies at bargain prices makes sense.* On average, this is what the magic formula does. *Second, it can take Mr. Market several years to recognize a bargain.* Therefore, the magic formula strategy requires patience. The information that follows in this section is merely additional commentary on these two points.

This appendix includes background information about the magic formula for those with a higher level of understanding of financial statements. It also compares the logic and results of the magic formula strategy with other studies and methods that have demonstrated an ability to beat the market.

# The Magic Formula

The magic formula ranks companies based on two factors: *return on capital* and *earnings yield*. These factors can be measured in several different ways. The measures chosen for the study in this book are described in more detail as follows:*

## 1. Return on Capital

EBIT/(Net Working Capital + Net Fixed Assets)

Return on capital was measured by calculating the ratio of pre-tax operating earnings (EBIT) to *tangible capital*

*For purposes of the study, earnings-related numbers were based on the latest 12-month period, balance sheet items were based on the most recent balance sheet, and market prices were based on the most recent closing price. Utilities, financial stocks and companies where we could not be certain that the information in the database was timely or complete were eliminated. Adjustments were also made for certain non-interest bearing liabilities. The study was structured so that an average of 30 stocks was held during the study period. Stocks with only limited liquidity were eliminated from the study. Market capitalizations were determined based on 2003 dollars. Both the number of companies in each decile as well as the number of companies in each market capitalization group fluctuated as the number of companies in the database varied during the study period.

*employed* (Net Working Capital + Net Fixed Assets). This ratio was used rather than the more commonly used ratios of *return on equity* (ROE, earnings/equity) or *return on assets* (ROA, earnings/assets) for several reasons.

EBIT (or *earnings before interest and taxes*) was used in place of reported earnings because companies operate with different levels of debt and differing tax rates. Using operating earnings before interest and taxes, or EBIT, allowed us to view and compare the operating earnings of different companies without the distortions arising from differences in tax rates and debt levels. For each company, it was then possible to compare actual earnings from operations (EBIT) to the cost of the assets used to produce those earnings (tangible capital employed).*

Net Working Capital + Net Fixed Assets (or tangible capital employed) was used in place of *total assets* (used in an ROA calculation) or *equity* (used in an ROE calculation). The idea here was to figure out how much capital is actually needed to conduct the company's business. Net working capital was used because a company has to fund its receivables and inventory (excess cash not needed to conduct the business was excluded from this calculation) but does not

---

*For purposes of the study and in the interest of simplicity, it was assumed that depreciation and amortization expense (noncash charges against earnings) were roughly equal to maintenance capital spending requirements (cash expenses not charged against earnings). It was, therefore, assumed that EBITDA − Maintenance Cap/Expenditures = EBIT.

have to lay out money for its payables, as these are effectively an interest-free loan (short-term interest-bearing debt was excluded from current liabilities for this calculation). In addition to working capital requirements, a company must also fund the purchase of fixed assets necessary to conduct its business, such as real estate, plant, and equipment. The

---

NOTE: *Intangible assets,* specifically *goodwill,* were excluded from the tangible capital employed calculations. Goodwill usually arises as a result of an acquisition of another company. The cost of an acquisition in excess of the tangible assets acquired is usually assigned to a goodwill account. In order to conduct its future business, the acquiring company usually only has to replace tangible assets, such as plant and equipment. Goodwill is a historical cost that does not have to be constantly replaced. Therefore, in most cases, return on tangible capital alone (excluding goodwill) will be a more accurate reflection of a business's return on capital going forward. The ROE and ROA calculations used by many investment analysts are therefore often distorted by ignoring the difference between *reported* equity and assets and *tangible* equity and assets in addition to distortions due to differing tax rates and debt levels.

depreciated net cost of these fixed assets was then added to the net working capital requirements already calculated to arrive at an estimate for tangible capital employed.

## 2. Earnings Yield

### EBIT/Enterprise Value

Earnings yield was measured by calculating the ratio of pre-tax operating earnings (EBIT) to *enterprise value* (market value of equity* + net interest-bearing debt). This ratio was used rather than the more commonly used *P/E ratio* (price/earnings ratio) or *E/P ratio* (earnings/price ratio) for several reasons. The basic idea behind the concept of earnings yield is simply to figure out how much a business earns relative to the purchase price of the business.

Enterprise value was used instead of merely the *price* of equity (i.e., *total market capitalization,* share price multiplied by shares outstanding) because enterprise value takes into account both the price paid for an equity stake in a business as well as the debt financing used by a company to help generate operating earnings. By using EBIT (which looks at actual operating earnings before interest expense and taxes) and comparing it to enterprise value, we can calculate the

---

*Including preferred equity.

pre-tax earnings yield on the full purchase price of a business (i.e., pre-tax operating earnings relative to the price of
equity plus any debt assumed). This allows us to put companies with different levels of debt and different tax rates on
an equal footing when comparing earnings yields.

For example, in the case of an office building purchased
for $1 million with an $800,000 mortgage and $200,000 in
equity, the price of equity is $200,000 but the enterprise
value is $1 million. If the building generates EBIT (earnings
before interest and taxes) of $100,000, then EBIT/EV or
the pre-tax earnings yield would be 10 percent ($100,000/
$1,000,000). However, the use of debt can greatly skew
apparent returns from the purchase of these same assets
when only the price of equity is considered. Assuming an
interest rate of 6 percent on an $800,000 mortgage and a 40
percent corporate tax rate, the pre-tax earnings yield on our
equity purchase price of $200,000 would appear to be 26
percent.* As debt levels change, this pre-tax earnings yield

---

*$100,000 in EBIT less $48,000 in interest expense equals $52,000 in pretax
income. $52,000/$200,000 equals 26 percent. The E/P (earnings/price), or
after-tax earnings yield, would be 15.6 percent ($100,000 in EBIT less
$48,000 in interest less $20,800 in income tax equals $31,200 in after-tax
income; $31,200/$200,000 equals 15.6 percent). This 15.6 percent return
would be more comparable to looking at an EBIT/EV after-tax yield of 6 percent (i.e., looking at EBIT as if fully taxed, or net operating profit after tax
divided by EV; *it is important to note that the fully taxed EBIT to enterprise value of
6 percent would be the earnings yield ratio used to measure investment alternatives versus the risk-free 10-year government bond yield, not the EBIT/EV ratio of 10 percent*).

on equity would keep changing, yet the $1 million cost of the building and the $100,000 EBIT generated by that building would remain unchanged. In other words, P/E and E/P are greatly influenced by changes in debt levels and tax rates, while EBIT/EV is not.

---

Consider two companies, Company A and Company B. They are actually the same company (i.e., the same sales, the same operating earnings, the same everything) except that Company A has no debt and Company B has $50 in debt (at a 10 percent interest rate). All information is per share.

|  | **Company A** | **Company B** |
|---|---|---|
| Sales | $100 | $100 |
| EBIT | 10 | 10 |
| Interest exp. | 0 | 5 |
| Pre-tax income | 10 | 5 |
| Taxes (@40%) | 4 | 2 |
| Net income | $6 | $3 |

The price of Company A is $60 per share. The price of Company B is $10 per share. Which is cheaper?

Let's see. The P/E of Company A is 10 ($60/6 = 10). The P/E of Company B is 3.33 ($10/3). The E/P, or earnings yield, of Company A is 10 percent (6/60), while the earnings yield of Company B is 30 percent (3/10). So which is cheaper? The answer is obvious. Company B has a P/E of only 3.33 and an earnings yield of 30 percent. That looks much cheaper than Company A's P/E of 10 and earnings yield of only 10 percent. So Company B is clearly cheaper, right?

Not so fast. Let's look at EBIT/EV for both companies. They are the same! To a buyer of the whole company, would it matter whether you paid *$10 per share for the company and owed another $50 per share* or you paid $60 and owed nothing? It is the same thing! *You would be buying $10 worth of EBIT for $60, either way!**

|                              | Company A        | Company B         |
| ---------------------------- | ---------------- | ----------------- |
| Enterprise value (price + debt) | 60 + 0 = $60  | 10 + 50 = $60     |
| EBIT                         | 10               | 10                |

*For example, whether you pay $200,000 for a building and assume an $800,000 mortgage or pay $1 million up front, it should be the same to you. The building costs $1 million either way!

# A Random Walk Spoiled

For many years, academics have debated whether it is possible to find bargain-priced stocks other than by chance. This notion, sometimes loosely referred to as the *random walk* or *efficient market* theory, suggests that for the most part, the stock market is very efficient at taking in all publicly available information and setting stock prices. That is, through the interaction of knowledgeable buyers and sellers, the market does a pretty good job of pricing stocks at "fair" value. This theory, along with the failure of most professional managers to beat the market averages over the long term,* has understandably led to the movement toward *indexing,* a cost-effective strategy designed to merely match the market's return.

Of course, over the years, many studies have attempted to identify strategies that *can* beat the market. But these studies have often been criticized on numerous grounds.

*Both before and after management fees and expenses.

These include:

1. The study beat the market because the data used to select stocks weren't really available to investors at the time the selections took place (a.k.a. *look-ahead bias*).

2. The study was biased because the database used in the study had been "cleaned up" and excluded companies that later went bankrupt, making the study results look better than they really were (a.k.a. *survivorship bias*).

3. The study included very small companies that couldn't have been purchased at the prices listed in the database and uncovered companies too small for professionals to buy.

4. The study did not outperform the market by a significant amount after factoring in transaction costs.

5. The study picked stocks that were in some way "riskier" than the market, and that's why performance was better.

6. The stock selection strategy was based on back-testing many different stock selection strategies until one was found that worked (a.k.a. *data mining*).

7. The stock selection strategies used to beat the market included knowledge gained from previous "market-beating" studies that was not available at

the time the stock purchases were made in the study.

Luckily, the magic formula study doesn't appear to have had *any* of these problems. A newly released database from Standard & Poor's Compustat, called "Point in Time," was used. This database contains the exact information that was available to Compustat customers on each date tested during the study period. The database goes back 17 years, the time period selected for the magic formula study. By using only this special database, it was possible to ensure that no look-ahead or survivorship bias took place.

Further, the magic formula worked for both small- and large-capitalization stocks, provided returns far superior to the market averages, and achieved those returns while taking on much *lower risk* than the overall market (no matter how that risk was measured). Consequently, small size, high transaction costs, and added risk do not appear to be reasonable grounds for questioning the validity of the magic formula results. As for data mining and using academic research not available at the time of stock selection, this did not take place, either. In fact, the two factors used for the magic formula study were actually the first two factors tested. Simply, a *high earnings yield* combined with a *high return on capital* were the two factors we judged to be most important when analyzing a company *before* the magic formula study was conducted. In sum, despite its obvious simplicity and the usual objections, the magic formula appears to work. It works well even when compared to much more sophisticated strategies used in some of the best market-beating research completed to date.

Yet, in one sense, the success of the magic formula strategy should not be a surprise. Simple methods for beating the market have been well known for quite some time. Many studies over the years have confirmed that *value-oriented* strategies beat the market over longer time horizons. Several different measures of value have been shown to work. These strategies include, but are not limited to, selecting stocks based upon low ratios of price to book value, price to earnings, price to cash flow, price to sales, and/or price to dividends. Similar to the results found in the magic formula study, these simple value strategies do not always work. However, measured over longer periods, they do. Though these strategies have been well documented over many years, most individual and professional investors do not have the patience to use them. Apparently, the long periods of underperformance make them difficult—and, for some professionals, impractical—to implement.

Another problem with these simple methods is that, though they work well, they work far better with smaller- and medium-capitalization stocks than with larger stocks. This should not be surprising, either. Companies that are too small for professionals to buy and that are not large enough to generate sufficient commission revenue to justify analyst coverage are more likely to be ignored or misunderstood. As a result, they are more likely to present opportunities to find bargain-priced stocks. This was the case in the magic formula study. The formula achieved the greatest performance with the smallest-capitalization stocks studied.

However, this good performance cannot be reasonably attributed to a small-cap effect because small-capitalization stocks did not appreciably outperform large caps during the study period. Dividing our universe of stocks into deciles by market capitalization during the 17-year study period, the smallest 10 percent of stocks provided returns of 12.1 percent, while the largest 10 percent of stocks returned 11.9 percent. The next deciles were similarly close: 12.2 percent for the next smallest and 11.9 percent for the next largest.

But the whole issue of whether small-capitalization stocks outperform large-capitalization stocks is not particularly relevant. It seems clear that there is a greater opportunity to find bargains (and overpriced stocks, for that matter) in the small-cap arena both because there are more stocks to choose from and because smaller stocks are more likely to be lightly analyzed and, as a result, more likely to be mispriced. In a sense, it is just easier for simple methods like price/book screens and the magic formula to find bargain stocks among these smaller-capitalization stocks.

However, where the magic formula parts ways with previous market-beating studies, whether simple or sophisticated, is that for larger stocks (market caps over $1 billion) the results for the magic formula remain incredibly robust. Other methods do not fare nearly as well. For example, during our study period, the most widely used measure to identify value and growth stocks, price to book value, did not discriminate particularly strongly between winners and losers for these larger stocks. The best-ranked decile of low price/book stocks (cheapest 10 percent) beat the worst-ranked decile of high price/book stocks (most expensive 10 percent) by only 2 percent per year.*

In comparison, the magic formula strategy did much better. The best-ranked decile of magic formula stocks (cheapest 10 percent) beat the worst-ranked decile (most expensive 10 percent) by over 14 percent per year on average during the 17-year study. The best decile returned 18.88 percent, the worst returned 4.66 percent, while the market average for this universe of over $1 billion stocks

---

*This is 13.72 percent for the lowest price/book decile to 11.51 percent for the highest price/book decile. The market average for this group was 11.64 percent.

was 11.7 percent. In truth, this is not surprising. While having a low price relative to the historical cost of assets may be an *indication* that a stock is cheap, high *earnings* relative to price and to the historical cost of assets are much more direct measures of cheapness and *should* work better. Of course, these two factors are the ones used in the magic formula study.

One of the most significant recent studies, conducted by Joseph Piotroski at the University of Chicago,* took price/book analysis one step further. Piotroski observed that while low price/book stocks beat the market on average, less than half of the stocks selected following this strategy actually outperformed the market. By using simple and readily available accounting metrics, Piotroski wondered whether he could improve the results of a generic price/book strategy. Piotroski rated the top quintile of low price/book stocks (i.e., the cheapest 20 percent) using nine different measures of financial health. These included measures of profitability, operating efficiency, and balance sheet strength. The results over the 21-year study were spectacular . . . with one exception.

For larger stocks, it didn't really work. For the largest

*Piotroski, J. "Value Investing: The Use of Historical Financial Statements to Separate Winners from Losers," *Journal of Accounting Research*, vol. 38, supplement, 2000.

one-third of stocks by market capitalization,* the highest-ranked stocks on Piotroski's nine-point scale *did not* significantly outperform the average low price/book stock.[†] This is not surprising, either. As already mentioned, it's just easier to find mispriced stocks among smaller- and mid-capitalization issues.

But this relative inability for market-beating methods to work with larger-cap stocks is not unique. Even very sophisticated market-beating strategies, while showing excellent results in general, do not fare nearly as well as the relatively simple magic formula in the large-cap universe.[‡] For example, some of the best work done to date on sophisticated factor models was completed by Robert Haugen and Nardin Baker.[§] Professor Haugen actually started an advisory business based on the excellent results achieved in this groundbreaking paper.

Essentially, instead of the two factors used in the magic formula strategy, Haugen developed a sophisticated model using 71 factors that supposedly help predict

---

*This is equivalent in the magic formula study to stocks with market capitalizations over approximately $700 million.

[†]Though Piotroski's "lowest"-ranked large-cap stocks did do poorly relative to other low price/book stocks, his ranking system selected a total of only 34 low-ranked stocks over 21 years.

[‡]Or in the small-cap universe.

[§]Haugen, R., and N. Baker, "Commonality in the Determinants of Expected Stock Returns," *Journal of Financial Economics,* Summer 1996.

how stocks will do in the future. These 71 factors evaluate stocks based on "risk, liquidity, financial structure, profitability, price history and analysts' estimates." Based on a complicated weighting of all of these different factors, Haugen's model predicts future returns for each stock. Historical "expected returns" for the stocks in the 3,000+ stock universe evaluated by Haugen's model have been posted on his web site, covering the period from February 1994 through November 2004. We decided to test Haugen's model to see whether it worked for large-capitalization stocks (those with a market capitalization over $1 billion in 2004 dollars).

It did. The results were quite spectacular. Over this 10+-year period, the market average for the large-cap universe tested returned 9.38 percent. But buying the highest-ranked stocks (best-ranked decile) based on Haugen's 71-factor model returned +22.98 percent. The lowest-ranked stocks (worst-ranked decile) actually lost 6.91 percent. This amounts to a spread of almost 30 percent between best and worst! This assumed that stocks were held for only one month and then reranked at the end of each month. Of course, though these results were great, the magic formula did better!

Over the same 10+-year period, the highest-ranked stocks (best-ranked decile) based on the magic formula two-factor model returned +24.25 percent. The worst-ranked stocks (worst-ranked decile) *lost* 7.91 percent.

This amounts to a spread from best to worst of over 32 percent! Though the results from the magic formula strategy were somewhat better (and easier to achieve) than the results from the 71-factor model used by Haugen, the performance of both methods was excellent and quite comparable. But here's the thing. Most people don't (and shouldn't) invest by buying stocks and holding them for only one month. Besides the huge amount of time, transaction costs, and tax expense involved, this is essentially a *trading* strategy, not really a practical long-term investment strategy. So what happens if we change our test and hold each portfolio for one year?*

Actually, something very interesting occurs. Haugen's 71-factor model still does well: the best-ranked decile returns +12.55 percent (versus 9.38 percent for the market) and the worst-ranked decile returns +6.92 percent. The spread from high to low is down to 5.63 percent. If we hadn't just seen the one-month returns, this would still look pretty good. But what happens with the magic formula? The best-ranked decile returns +18.43 percent and the worst-ranked decile returns

---

*Portfolios were purchased every month during the 10-year period, and each portfolio was held for 1 year, so more than 120 separate portfolios were tested for each strategy.

+1.49 percent—a spread of almost 17 percent between best and worst! That's pretty good no matter how you look at it. Here's something else that's interesting. The worst return during those 10+ years for following the Haugen strategy for 36 months straight (with annual turnover) was −43.1 percent. The worst 36-month period for the magic formula was +14.3 percent. Not only that, the magic formula used 69 fewer factors and a lot less math!*

So, here's the point. The magic formula appears to perform very well. I think and hope it will continue to perform well in the future. I also hope that, just as Mark Twain aptly referred to golf as "a good walk spoiled," perhaps someday the random walk will finally be considered spoiled as well.[†]

---

*Professor Haugen does not suggest buying the top 10% of his highest rated stocks in one portfolio or holding stocks for one year. Also, the losses for the worst 36 month return for the theoretical "top 10%" Haugen portfolio were similar to the overall market's loss during that period. The statistics listed were compiled for comparison purposes with the magic formula portfolio using only those stocks that were included in both the Haugen and magic formula over $1 billion universe.

[†]On second thought, who am I kidding? I hope it lives forever!